What if we do **nOthing?**

GLOBAL WARMING

Neil Morris

W

FRANKLIN WATTS

LONDON•SYDNEY

First published in 2007 by
Franklin Watts
338 Euston Road
London NW1 3BH

Franklin Watts Australia
Hachette Children's Books
Level 17/207 Kent St, Sydney, NSW 2000

Produced by Arcturus Publishing Limited
26/27 Bickels Yard, 151-153 Bermondsey Street, London SE1 3HA

Series concept: Alex Woolf
Editor: Jenni Rainford
Designer: Peta Phipps
Consultant: Rob Bowden

Picture Credits
Corbis: 4 (NASA/Corbis), 8 (James L. Amos/CORBIS), 11 and cover (Hans
Strand/CORBIS), 12 (Torleif Svensson/CORBIS), 15 (Roger Wood/CORBIS),
19 (NOAA/ZUMA/Corbis), 20 (Rob Bowden/ EASI-Images), 23 (Scott T. Smith/CORBIS),
24 and cover (Nic Bothma/epa/Corbis), 29 (Franz Marc Frei/Corbis),
35 (Ed Kashi/Corbis), 36 (Klaus Hackenberg/zefa/Corbis), 39 (Yann Arthus-
Bertrand/CORBIS), 40 (Jon Hicks/CORBIS), 43 (Da Silva Peter/Corbis Sygma),
44 (CHRISTINNE MUSCHI/Reuters/Corbis).
FLPA: 30 (Michael and Patricia Fogden/Minden Pictures/FLPA).
Rex Features: 7 (Image Source/Rex Features).
TopFoto: 16 (Topfoto), 27 (UNEP/Topfoto), 32 and cover (AP/Topfoto).

A CIP catalogue record for this book is available from the British Library

Dewey Decimal Classification Number: 363.738'74

ISBN: 978 0 7496 6964 5

Printed in China

Contents

CHAPTER 1

Changing Climate

It is March 2020. World leaders and their environment ministers are gathered in Tokyo for an important summit meeting. They have travelled to the world's largest city, but the presidents, prime ministers and officials are not there to talk about the world's expanding population or urban development. They have come to discuss what the nations of the world can do to limit a problem that is having serious consequences everywhere. The issue under discussion is global warming.

Many years earlier, after countless meetings about global warming, in 1992 the United Nations held an 'Earth Summit' in Rio de Janeiro. Five years later, the world's representatives met in Kyoto, and many nations signed an agreement – called the Kyoto Protocol – to work towards slowing down global warming. This agreement came into effect in 2005, and by the beginning of the following year 163 countries had ratified it.

What is global warming?

Global warming is a gradual rise in the temperature of the Earth. Scientists believe that the Earth's temperature has gone up and down over millions of years. For example, there have been several glacial periods (ice ages), when many parts of the world were much colder than they are now. These periods alternated with shorter, interglacial periods, when the ice melted and the climate was generally warmer. The last ice age ended 20–10,000 years ago.

This satellite image of planet Earth shows how it is lit by the Sun. The Sun's energy gives us light and heat - without it, life on Earth would not be possible.

Such changes in climate were caused by natural forces, with no influence from humans in prehistoric and ancient times. But experts think that the temperature rise in recent times – especially in the late 20th and early 21st centuries – has been influenced or even caused by human activities.

Polluting our world

During the last century people all over the world have burned more and more fossil fuels – coal, oil and natural gas. These fuels are non-renewable: there are finite supplies of them, so they will eventually run out. They also release pollutants, including carbon dioxide and other gases, which contribute towards global warming.

The problem is that most regions of the world are dependent on fossil fuels for their energy needs. They are used in power stations to make electricity and as petrol and oil in cars and other vehicles (see Chapter 7). In 1997, delegates at Kyoto concentrated on getting nations to reduce the amount of harmful gases released into the atmosphere by our overdependence on fossil fuels. By 2020, they will know whether what they agreed achieved the effect they wanted – a true reduction in global emissions of greenhouse gases into the Earth's atmosphere and, ultimately, a limit to global warming.

GLOBAL TEMPERATURE RISE

The red line on this chart shows the average yearly temperature on Earth between 1860 and 2000. The black line shows the average yearly temperature on Earth between 1961 and 1990. Over 140 years the average temperature has risen by 0.8°C.

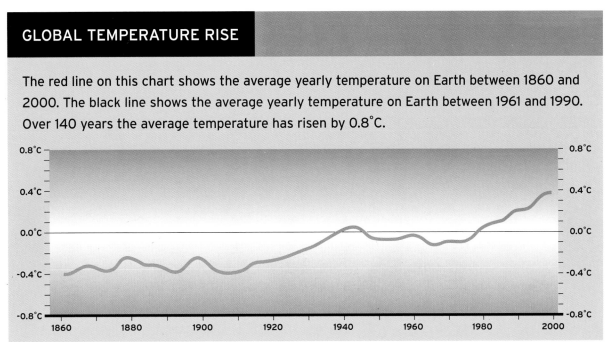

Source: Intergovernmental Panel on Climate Change

The greenhouse effect

The Sun's rays heat the Earth's land and sea. But more than one-third of the Sun's energy bounces back off the Earth's surface, like light reflected by a mirror, and moves back through the atmosphere towards space. However, certain gases, water vapour and particles in the atmosphere prevent the Sun's energy from escaping by absorbing some of the heat. It is similar to the way in which glass traps heat inside a greenhouse, keeping it warm. For this reason the gases' action in the atmosphere is called the 'greenhouse effect'.

The natural greenhouse effect makes a big difference to the temperature of our planet. Without it, the average temperature of the Earth's surface today would be about $-18°C$. But with the blanketing effect of the greenhouse gases, the actual average temperature is about $15°C$ – comfortable for humans to exist.

THE MAIN GREENHOUSE GASES

gas	source
Carbon dioxide (CO_2)	Found in nature, but also released by burning any substance that contains carbon, such as coal, petrol and wood
Methane (CH_4)	The main component of natural gas, but also released by landfill waste sites, livestock farms and rice paddies; it absorbs 23 times as much heat as CO_2
Nitrous oxide (N_2O)	Found in nature, but also released by industry and agriculture
Ozone (O_3)	Mostly in the upper atmosphere (the ozone layer), but warming also comes from ozone in the lower atmosphere
Water vapour	The biggest contributor to the natural greenhouse effect
Halocarbons	Synthetic chemicals that include a group of chlorofluorocarbons (CFCs), which used to be found in refrigerators, aerosols and packaging materials, and the less destructive hydrochlorofluorocarbons (HCFCs)
Sulphur hexafluoride (SF_6)	Produced in some industrial processes and mainly used in the electronics industry for insulation

Human action

The greenhouse effect has been working for millions of years, long before human beings existed on Earth. In recent years, however, our increasing use of fossil fuels and greater industrialization has released much larger quantities of greenhouse gases into the atmosphere. This has upset the natural balance and caused what scientists call an 'enhanced greenhouse effect'. The effect is stronger, trapping more of the Sun's energy and causing global warming.

The most important greenhouse gas is carbon dioxide (CO_2), which is produced naturally by animals as they convert food into energy. On Earth, plants need carbon dioxide to live and grow, just as we need the oxygen that they give off. But burning fossil fuels for energy and cutting down forests for urban development also give off large amounts of carbon dioxide. Scientists have calculated that CO_2 has caused up to 70 percent of the enhanced greenhouse effect.

This oil refinery turns crude oil into petrol and many other substances. During this process, carbon dioxide and other harmful gases are released into the atmosphere.

DEBATE

You are in charge

You are a government minister addressing a climate conference. Some action points have been suggested. What would you suggest all countries make their priority?

■ Set a target for reducing emission of greenhouse gases.
■ Concentrate on reducing the emissions of carbon dioxide.
■ Bring in programmes to stop forests being cut down.
■ Increase use of renewable energy sources, such as wind, water and solar power.
■ Give incentives to people to use less energy, such as paying less tax on cars that use less petrol and travelling by public transport.

CHAPTER 2

Icy Meltdown

Tulugaq was born in an Inuit community in 1980. Now he's forty years old, and he looks back at how much the community on Baffin Island, in the Canadian territory of Nunavut, has changed since he was a boy. Now, in 2020, the winter is shorter, the ice is thinner and he has to work much harder. That's because, as global warming takes its toll on traditional life, it is more difficult to find the seals that his family has hunted for centuries. Tulugaq and his wife sell soapstone carvings of seals, bears and caribou to tourists. Tulugaq wonders whether his children will stay in this community, or even in their Inuit homeland.

Arctic effects

Scientists have recorded the effects of global warming in the Arctic region around the North Pole for many years. That is because they are easy to see. As the region warms up, the ice melts, becoming thinner in some places and disappearing altogether in others. Centuries ago, when explorers searched for a way from Europe to Asia, they tried to sail through the Bering Strait from the Arctic to the Pacific Ocean. For hundreds of years, they were prevented from achieving this by the ice. In 1879, Swedish captain Nils Nordenskjöld successfully sailed through the North-East Passage (across the top of Siberia) and the Bering Strait. Today, Russian ice-breakers keep the channel free of ice so that ships can

The Greenland ice sheet is melting. Experts predict that it may take 1,000 years for the sheet to disappear completely.

pass through. But by 2020, according to the US Office of Naval Research, the North-East Passage and the North-West Passage (across the top of Canada) will be free of ice all year round.

Polar ice mass

Global warming is melting the Arctic ice on both land and sea. More than two-thirds of the Arctic Ocean is frozen all year round, but since 1980, this polar ice mass has been getting smaller by 9 percent per decade. That's nearly 1 percent each year. The ice mass is still up to 50 metres thick in some places, but scientists say it has thinned by between 15 and 40 percent since the mid-1970s.

On land

Arctic ice is also melting on land. This includes the great ice sheet that covers about four-fifths of the world's largest island, Greenland. The ice is up to 3.2 kilometres thick in places, but research shows that it may be thinning at up to 10 metres per year. This is ten times more than previously thought. Higher temperatures may also affect Arctic permafrost, too. At the moment, this permanently frozen ground covers more than 10 million square kilometres. But by 2020 a quarter of this area may no longer be permafrost.

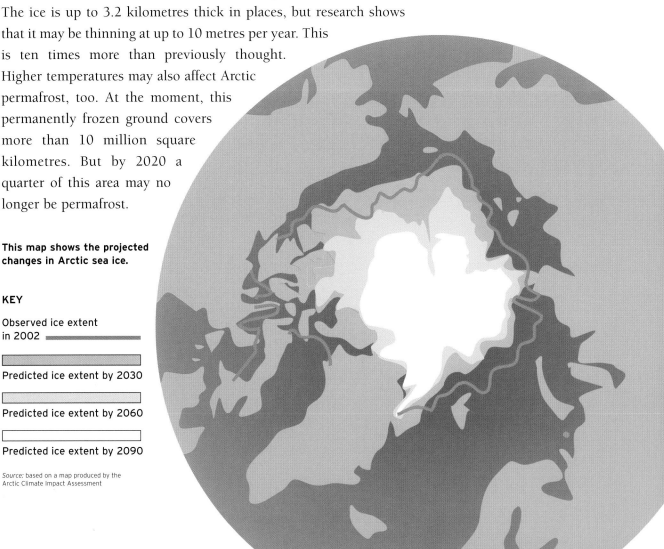

This map shows the projected changes in Arctic sea ice.

KEY

Observed ice extent in 2002

Predicted ice extent by 2030

Predicted ice extent by 2060

Predicted ice extent by 2090

Source: based on a map produced by the Arctic Climate Impact Assessment

Albedo effect

The Arctic region may be warming up more than other parts of the world because of the albedo effect. This happens because snow and ice are white and so reflect up to 90 percent of sunlight, compared with 45 percent for sandy desert, 20 percent for green fields, 8 percent for brown earth and just 3.5 percent for oceans. Our planet's average albedo is 39 percent – less than half that of the polar regions.

As ice melts, it exposes darker land or sea, which is less reflective and so absorbs more heat. As the land heats up, more ice at the edges melts, and more land or sea is exposed, and the cycle continues, building up over a period of years. It is impossible to stop. According to 2005 forecasts, the Arctic region could warm three times as much as the rest of the world in the next few decades.

Indigenous people

Climate change affects everyone but it is particularly important to the people of the Arctic. In 1996 the eight Arctic nations – Canada, Denmark (for Greenland and the Faroe Islands), Finland, Iceland, Norway, Russia, Sweden and the United States (for Alaska) – formed an Arctic Council to protect their environment. The Council represents the interests of about 4 million people, including the Inuit of Greenland, Canada, Alaska and Russia, and the Saami (or Lapps) of northern Norway, Sweden and Finland. Part of the Council's work is to keep monitoring the Arctic environment, to see how it is affected by

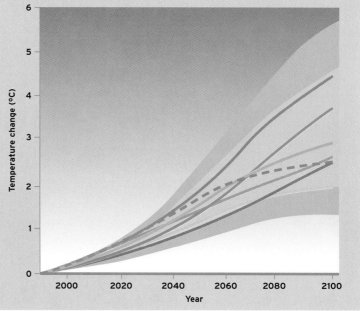

PROJECTED INCREASE IN WORLD TEMPERATURE

The range of curving lines shows how scientists' predictions vary according to different levels of increase in greenhouse gas emissions. The lowest curve is based on little or no increase, and the upper curves on higher increases. By 2020 the temperature might go up by between 0.3°C and 0.8°C, and by 2100, by between 1.4°C and 5.8°C. The dotted line shows the average prediction.

Source: Intergovernmental Panel on Climate Change

global warming. Scientists constantly check the coverage and thickness of ice, changes in temperature and the health and movement of Arctic animals.

If the world warmed up so much that the Arctic ice melted completely, polar bears could be extinct within 100 years.

Living on the pack ice

Polar bears live only in the Arctic, where they feed mainly on seals. They have always followed the ice as it moves and retreats during the summer. They hunt seals by looking for holes in the ice, where the seals come up for air. When the pack ice breaks up, polar bears swim to floating islands of ice and pounce on seals resting there. Polar bears could be greatly affected if global warming causes the reduction in sea ice that many experts predict. If the ice continues to melt at current rates, polar bears may have to change their way of life in order to survive.

Bears in the southern limits such as Hudson Bay are most at risk. Some experts have suggested that the bears could adapt to a less icy habitat. They could become more like brown bears in Alaska, which hunt salmon in rivers and streams, and small mammals on land. Others fear they could simply die out (see Chapter 5).

Frozen continent

The difference between the Arctic and the frozen continent of Antarctica is that most Antarctic ice lies on top of land. The ice cap is up to 4.8 kilometres thick in places. The Antarctic ice sheets are so huge that more than two-thirds of the world's fresh water is locked up in its ice. The continent has no indigenous people, but a resident population of international scientists use Antarctica as an important base for studying changes in the climate.

They have found that ice in the western part of Antarctica is thinning by an average of about 10 centimetres per year. But owing to rising temperatures, in some places it is thinning by up to 4 metres per year. Some of this thinning may be caused by volcanic heat rising up beneath the rock on which the ice rests. In 2002, a

This photo shows snow and ice on top of Mount Kilimanjaro, Africa's highest mountain. It lies near the Equator, in Tanzania. The mountain has lost one-third of its ice in the past 12 years, and scientists believe that by 2020 its icy cap may have totally melted.

large part of the Larsen ice shelf, at the edge of the Antarctic Peninsula, broke up completely in just over a month. Because of this, glaciers that make their way to the sea in this region flowed up to six times faster. A scientist at the US National Snow and Ice Data Center said, "If anyone was waiting to find out whether Antarctica would respond quickly to climate warming, I think the answer is yes."

The world's glaciers

Glaciers are found in many other parts of the world, especially in high mountain ranges. When Glacier National Park, in the Rocky Mountains of northern Montana, USA, was made into a national park in 1910, it had about 150 glaciers. Because of rising temperatures during the 20th century, it now has 37 named glaciers, and they have all shrunk dramatically in recent decades. In that time, for example, the park's Sperry Glacier has shrunk from an area of more than 3 square kilometres to less than 1 square kilometre. A similar situation has been found in the European Alps and the South American Andes.

Shorter winters

Scientists have discovered that winters have become shorter in recent decades, which may be another result of global warming. Records show that a lake in the US state of Wisconsin froze over for 119 days of the year more than a century ago, whereas in the early 21st century, it froze for just 80 days. The world's deepest lake – Lake Baikal in Russia – freezes over for 23 days fewer than it did 100 years ago.

DEBATE

You are in charge
You represent a local community of indigenous people in one of the Arctic countries. You have an appointment with the environment minister of your country. Explain how global warming concerns you. What evidence could you use to convince the minister to take the issue seriously?

CHAPTER 3

Rising Seas

Like millions of their fellow Bangladeshis, Shamsur, his wife Jakia, and their family are rice farmers. Twenty years ago, they used to get three crops a year from their small plot, using the seasonal rains to their advantage. But now, in 2020, times are very hard: their paddy fields are constantly under too much water, and the water contains too much salt from the sea. Shamsur and Jakia have moved their plot several times, but they do not know whether they will get permission from the agricultural authorities to move it again. The authorities know that Bangladesh is fast running out of usable farmland, making it difficult to feed its 210 million people.

A global issue

A warmer world means rising sea levels, and this has always been the case. About 130,000 years ago, before the start of the last ice age, the global temperature was a little higher than today – about 2°C warmer. Then the average sea level was 5 or 6 metres higher than today. But about 18,000 years ago, ice cover was very thick and the sea level was more than 100 metres lower than it is now – the Atlantic Ocean and North Sea were so low that Britain was joined by dry land to continental Europe.

PROJECTED RISE IN SEA LEVEL

The range of curving lines shows varying predictions according to different increases in greenhouse gas emissions. The lowest curve is based on little or no increase, and the upper curves on higher increases. By 2020 sea level might go up by between 2 cm and 10 cm, and by 2100 by between 10 cm and 90 cm. The dotted line shows the average prediction.

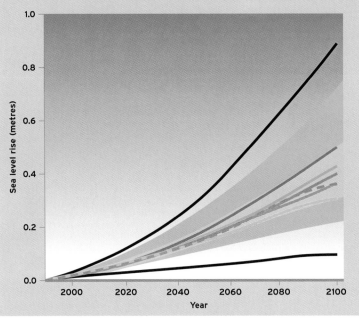

Source: Intergovernmental Panel on Climate Change

An Egyptian man rides his donkey across the Nile delta. If sea levels rise as scientists warn, this area is at great risk of total flooding from the Mediterranean Sea.

Warm water is less dense than cold water, so global warming makes the oceans expand. But much more importantly, melting ice turns to water, so the warming of the two polar regions, as well as glaciers around the world, will potentially have a huge impact on sea level.

Living near low-lying coasts and river deltas

According to an estimate by the National Geographic Society, more than 100 million of the world's population live on land that is less than 1 metre above present sea level. That land will disappear if the sea rises by 1 metre. According to current forecasts, it appears that the rise might be up to 10 centimetres by 2020, and up to 90 centimetres by 2100. What people living in the 22nd century can expect is more difficult to predict.

The world's river deltas are densely populated, and these areas may be hardest hit by any increase in sea levels. The Nile delta in northern Egypt and the Mississippi delta in the southern United States are particularly vulnerable. Sea-level rise in the Ganges delta of Bangladesh could be made worse by two other factors. The land there is subsiding due to land movements, and vast quantities of groundwater are being removed for drinking and irrigation. Experts say that in Bangladesh the effects could be equivalent to a rise in the sea level of 1 metre by 2050.

Low-lying islands

Some of the world's low-lying islands have already experienced the effects of a rise in sea level, and many people have been forced to move away from the coast or even leave their island. In the Pacific island country of Tuvalu, for example, where the sea level rose by 20–30 centimetres during the 20th century, people began leaving the small islands in 2001. It has been estimated that half a million people live on groups of small, low-lying islands around the world.

The Maldives are made up of about 1,200 small coral islands – 200 of which are inhabited – that form a chain more than 750 kilometres long in the Indian Ocean, to the south-west of India. Their total land area now is only 298 square kilometres – that's less than one-third of the size of New York City. Natural barrier reefs surround many

On the low-lying Maldives most of the islanders' income is generated through fishing and tourism. But as sea levels rise, and land disappears, fewer people will be able to live on the islands and tourists may no longer be able to visit them.

of the island atolls, but they will not be able to protect them from the rising sea. The highest point on the Maldives is currently just 2.4 metres above sea level.

The reality of what life might be like with rising sea levels was illustrated all too clearly to the Maldivians by the disastrous tsunami of 26 December 2004, when up to 40 percent of their land was under water at some point. Fortunately, most of the islanders live in Male, the nation's capital, which is protected by a high sea wall. Nevertheless, homes on 20 inhabited islands were completely destroyed, 15,000 Maldivians were made homeless, and 82 were killed. Sea level rise would be a gradual process, unlike a tsunami, so would be unlikely to lead to such death and destruction. However, it remains a serious threat, and the government has launched a 'Safe Islands' project, picking out five main islands that they will try to protect from rising seas.

Pacific islands

Many of the thousands of small Pacific islands are threatened by predicted rising sea levels. They include the Marshall Islands; a 0.5 metre rise in sea level would submerge more than three-quarters of the country's 181 square kilometre area.

The Marshall Islands and the Maldives are sharing ideas with other island groups, such as the Bahamas in the Atlantic. They are developing early-warning systems in case of a sudden rise in sea level, and looking at ways to help islanders protect their homes or relocate to other areas. In 1990, during a World Climate Conference in Geneva, the islands formed the Alliance of Small Island States (AOSIS), which now has over 40 members. At one of their regular meetings, the delegate for the Caribbean island of St Lucia said they had to take action on rising sea levels now: "If we wait for the proof, the proof will kill us".

What happens to the world's low-lying areas will depend on how much and how quickly world temperatures rise. Though the world's climate does go through natural periods of warming, the rate of current warming appears to be at least partly due to human influence.

TWENTY HOTTEST YEARS ON RECORD

The records of annual temperatures, which date back as far as 1880, show that 18 of the hottest years on record have occurred since the mid-1980s.

Rank	Year
=1	2005
=1	1998
3	2002
4	2003
5	2004
6	2001
7	1997
8	1990
9	1995
10	1999
11	2000
12	1991
13	1987
14	1988
15	1994
16	1983
17	1996
18	1944
19	1989
20	1993

Source: Union of Concerned Scientists

Flood defences

In Europe, figures show that the sea has risen by about 15 centimetres over the past 200 years. This rise has had a big effect on countries such as the Netherlands, which is one of the Low Countries (along with Belgium and Luxembourg). About half of the Netherlands' land lies below sea level. For centuries, the Dutch have built banks and dykes along their coast to keep out the sea and have reclaimed the land by draining seawater from flooded areas.

In 1953, storm surge waves crashed over the dykes and flooded a large coastal region. The Dutch government then built the 7-kilometre-long Dutch Sea Barrier, a series of strong dams with concrete piers and steel gates that allow water to pass the dam when they are open. The gates can be closed if there is a very high tide or severe storm. The Dutch also drained some areas, called polders, using windmills or pumps to transfer the water into drainage canals that led to rivers and back to the sea. Some polders are more than 6 metres below sea level.

Other countries can learn a great deal from the Dutch experience, but poorer countries, such as Bangladesh or the Maldives, would need financial help to build such defences.

DEBATE

You are in charge
You are a minister working for the international community and you are addressing a seminar on global accountability. Which nations would you argue should take responsibility for their CO_2 emissions? Should those nations help to pay the cost of protecting low-lying areas around the world against rising sea levels?

Disaster strikes

The Asian tsunami of December 2004 destroyed the sea defences of many areas around the Indian Ocean and took the lives of many thousands of people. In 2005 Hurricane Katrina caused a storm surge that breached the levee protecting New Orleans from Lake Pontchartrain, on the Gulf Coast of the United States. The storm passed 32 kilometres east of downtown New Orleans, destroying many buildings, flooding more than three-quarters of the city and killing more than 1,300 people. The damage was caused by the storm surge and the breach of coastal and river levees more than by the winds. Katrina was a clear warning that the potential increase in sea levels will have a dramatic effect on the lives of people living in such low-lying areas.

Tropical cyclones (generally called hurricanes in the western Atlantic; typhoons in the western Pacific; and cyclones in the Indian Ocean) form over warm oceans with a water temperature of at least 27°C. Many scientists believe that warmer oceans (see Chapter 6) will lead to more tropical cyclones, and this seems to be the case already in the western Atlantic, including the Caribbean Sea and Gulf of Mexico.

The year 2005 broke all records for storms in the western Atlantic region. There were 27 named storms (twice the recent average), 14 hurricanes and 7 major hurricanes (twice the recent average). Of the seven majors, three reached category-5 status (the highest, with wind speeds of more than 251 kilometres per hour), including Hurricane Katrina.

This satellite image shows Hurricane Katrina as it moved towards the Gulf Coast of the USA, in August 2005. The calm 'eye' in the middle of the hurricane is clearly visible, with thick clouds whirling around it.

CHAPTER 4

Human Health

It is 2020 and Emma, a successful British TV producer, has won an award for best sports documentary. The presentation ceremony is being held in Beijing. Emma has travelled all over the world making programmes, and is surprised to discover that she will now need to take anti-malaria tablets, mosquito spray and a net for her trip to northern China. Malaria is advancing ever northwards to previously unaffected regions.

Since human health is dependent on good environmental conditions and is linked to climate, experts believe that global warming will have a damaging effect in a number of different ways. Factors like air pollution, poor soil conditions and a lack of adequate food and water would increase health problems and the spread of disease.

Heat stress

It is anticipated that increasing temperatures may lead to greater numbers of cases of heat-related illness and even fatalities. Scientists warn that climate change may already be causing up to 160,000 deaths a year, and that heat-related fatalities could double by 2020.

This farmer in Rajasthan, India, is ploughing the dry scrubland, which is difficult for food plants and animals to survive on. Higher temperatures and drought would affect farmers all over the world, in both rich and poor regions.

In the summer of 2003, about 35,000 people died as a result of a record heatwave in Europe. The greatest number of deaths was in France, where nearly 15,000 people died. It was the hottest August on record in the northern hemisphere, and earlier in the year it had been even hotter in India. There, in May 2003, temperatures soared to 49°C and claimed more than 1,600 lives. People brought up in hot countries are generally more tolerant of heatwaves. Scientists say that people in London, especially the elderly, start to suffer at 22°C, while in the Greek capital of Athens, the figure is 26°C.

Heat stress mainly affects old, very young and chronically ill people. Out of over 2,000 people who died in the 2003 heatwave in the UK, 85 percent were aged 75 and over. And scientists point out that hotter summers will be followed by less cold winters, which may lead to fewer deaths due to extremes of cold. Nevertheless, according to the Earth Policy Institute of Washington, DC, heatwaves claim more lives each year than floods, tornadoes and hurricanes.

World food supply

Many people in developing countries farm the land and grow their own food, but often they simply cannot produce enough. The result is that at least 800 million people (12 percent of the world's population) are starving. If growing conditions are made more difficult in developing countries, for example by a hotter, drier climate, farmers will find life even more difficult. Aid agencies are trying to combat this problem by helping people to improve their own farming techniques.

It is predicted that by 2020 developing countries will be even more dependent on richer nations for staple cereal crops. Compared with 1988, the cereal deficit in developing countries will be three times as high. This is because rich, industrialized countries control the world food network, helping their own producers and keeping down the price they are prepared to pay for imported food. If global warming adds to the problem of food production, the rich nations will have to do more to help poor regions.

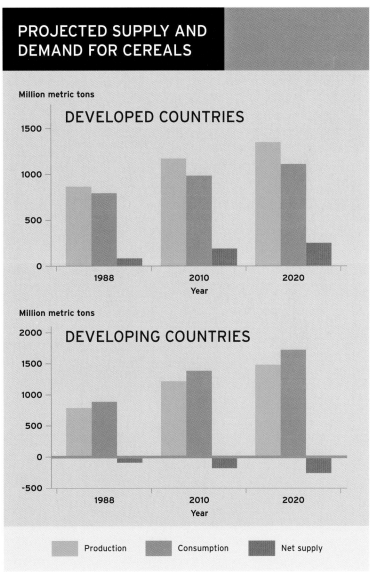

PROJECTED SUPPLY AND DEMAND FOR CEREALS

Million metric tons

DEVELOPED COUNTRIES

Million metric tons

DEVELOPING COUNTRIES

Production   Consumption   Net supply

Source: International Food Policy Research Institute

Increased spread of disease

A hotter climate may increase the risk of catching certain diseases. It can help bacteria to breed, so there could be more cases of complaints such as food poisoning. Serious waterborne bacterial diseases, such as cholera and typhoid, might also increase in countries such as Bangladesh – especially if global warming leads to wetter as well as warmer conditions in parts of the world that are already vulnerable to these diseases.

Diseases that are spread by mosquitoes and other insects – malaria, dengue fever, yellow fever and encephalitis – could become more common if warmer temperatures allow the parasites to live outside tropical regions. According to the World Health Organization, malaria is one of the world's most devastating diseases. Today, more people suffer from malaria than from any other disease. Owing mainly to the growth in population, the numbers affected and at risk are increasing all the time.

Climate studies and the future

In Africa and other malarial regions, a World Health Organization project called 'Roll Back Malaria' is providing people with sprays for their homes and bed nets treated with insecticide, as well as new

ANNUAL DEATHS CAUSED BY MALARIA IN 2002-03

region	no. of deaths	% of world total	no. of deaths of children under 5
Africa	1,136,000	89	802,000
North & South America	1,000	0.1	1,000
Southeast Asia	65,000	5	12,000
Europe	0	0	0
Eastern Mediterranean	59,000	5	37,000
Western Pacific	11,000	0.9	1,000
TOTAL	1,272,000	100	853,000

Source: World Health Organization

anti-malarial drugs. Also, climate experts are using computer models of changing weather patterns to predict outbreaks of malaria up to five months in advance. In Botswana, the National Malaria Control Programme has developed an early warning system. In neighbouring South Africa, scientists believe that if nothing is done, the numbers of those at high risk of contracting malaria will quadruple by 2020.

Whatever happens in terms of global warming, the future of all these diseases, including malaria, may vary greatly in different parts of the world. The number of cases will depend on many other factors, including the wealth and public health system of any particular region.

Water stress

Clean fresh water is essential to good health, so scientists are looking at how global warming might affect the world's water cycle. A rise in sea level may cause salt water to enter groundwater reserves and contaminate some freshwater supplies. At the same time, dry areas are expected to become drier. Many countries already suffer from water stress, particularly in North Africa and south-western and central Asia.

The term 'stress' refers to the proportion of available fresh water that is withdrawn for use. The World Water Council defines withdrawal of 10 percent as 'low water stress', 20 percent withdrawal is 'mid', 40 percent 'high' and 80 percent 'very high' water stress. In the 1990s about 1.7 billion people lived in mid- to very high-stressed regions. This number is expected to rise to about 5 billion (nearly 60 percent of the estimated world population) by 2025.

This person is wearing mosquito-proof headgear, designed to keep the insects away from the skin. Mosquitoes can pass on malaria when they bite people to feed on blood and moisture.

This Sudanese girl is carrying water from an aid camp. Safe drinking water is a precious resource throughout northern Africa and, as demand for water increases as the world's population grows, it may become even more scarce.

During the second half of the 20th century, worldwide water use tripled. In North America and Japan, people in residential areas used an average of 350 litres a day; in Europe, the figure was 200 litres; but in sub-Saharan Africa, the figure was just 10–20 litres. In 2003 the World Water Forum decided that the aim by 2020 should be 40 litres per person, per day worldwide.

Today, more than one in six people across the world lack access to safe drinking water. Between 2000 and 2020, the need for water will grow by about 26 percent. By 2020 the world's population is predicted to reach more than 8 billion, and by then up to two-thirds of the world's people may face shortages of clean fresh water. However, we don't know exactly how global warming will affect this situation, and in some regions it may lead to more rainfall.

Shrinking lakes

In the 1960s, Lake Chad covered an area of 23,000 square kilometres and spread across the borders of Chad, Niger, Nigeria and Cameroon in Africa. By 2005 it had shrunk to just 900 square kilometres, and its shores were all within the country of Chad. However, it has always been a seasonal lake, growing in size during the rainy season from July to September, and it was always shallow, with many parts clogged up by reeds and other plants.

The debate on global warming is complex because of disputes over what can be classed as 'evidence'. Scientists who believe that global warming is a serious threat argue that the changes in the world's lake sizes are hard evidence of climate change. But others argue that lake shrinkages are due to factors such as poor land and irrigation management. Scientists believe that thousands of years ago, Lake Chad may have been a vast inland sea, but they have also found evidence that it may well have dried out several times in the past thousand years. Historically, these changes would have been mainly the result of natural variations in the climate, but since the 1960s the lake has been receiving less water as its feeder rivers are used for irrigation of nearby cotton fields.

DEBATE

You are in charge
As an up-and-coming politician you represent a region where a large river dam is being planned, to supply domestic water and hydroelectricity. Your constituents ask you how global warming might affect the river and their water supplies in years to come – how would you reply?

Endangering Species

It is 2020 and Stef has just joined the Great Barrier Reef Marine Park Authority (GBRMPA), which is celebrating its 45th birthday. She is proud to work for an organization that is responsible for the care and development of a UNESCO World Heritage site, Australia's beautiful coral reefs. Stef's job is to check the permits of tourist operators, giving advice on any problems and making sure that they obey the regulations. Twenty years ago the Marine Park had 820 tourist operators and 1.8 million visitors to the reef. Now the figures are much higher but at the same time some of the reefs are dying because of rising sea temperatures.

Dwindling biodiversity

Global warming has an effect on ecosystems, and, therefore, the animals and plants that live within each habitat will begin to suffer. Scientists are concerned that this will lead to a decline in biodiversity – the variety of plant and animal life in a particular habitat.

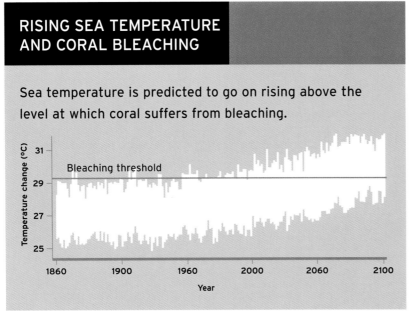

RISING SEA TEMPERATURE AND CORAL BLEACHING

Sea temperature is predicted to go on rising above the level at which coral suffers from bleaching.

Source: Marine and Freshwater Research

Conservationists warn that some species that are endangered now may even face extinction in the not-too-distant future.

The Intergovernmental Panel on Climate Change lists some species as being particularly threatened by global warming:

- mountain gorilla of Rwanda, D.R. Congo and Uganda
- amphibians of Central and South America
- spectacled bear of South America
- forest birds of Tanzania
- Bengal tiger of the Sundarban wetlands in India and Bangladesh
- polar bear of the Arctic
- penguins of the Antarctic

Coral bleaching

Global warming is already having a great effect on the world's coral reefs. This is shown by Australia's Great Barrier Reef, which is a series of coral reefs that stretch for more than 2,300 kilometres along the Queensland coast. This collection of reefs has more than 400 types of coral. These animals are coelenterates (in the same family as jellyfish), called polyps, and they make the limestone skeletons that build up the reef. But the polyps cannot exist without algae that live in their tissue, and it is these algae that are being specially affected by climate change. A rise in sea temperature (of, say, 1°C) causes the polyps to expel the algae, leading to a loss of colour, called bleaching. This generally happens at about 29.5°C. The average sea temperature around the Great Barrier Reef has been rising since the end of the 1990s (see chart), and is predicted to continue rising this century. If the temperature rise continues or increases (say, by 3°C), the coral will die.

Rising sea temperatures can also lead to coral disease, and these problems can affect fish – there are 1,500 species around the Reef – and other marine animals that live among the reefs. In 2002 the GBRMPA launched a monitoring programme that co-ordinates tour operators, researchers and the public to report cases of bleaching.

Just like the Great Barrier Reef, this coral reef off the Ryukyu Islands of Japan has been affected by bleaching in recent years.

Penguin populations

All species of penguin live in cold, southern waters, and several live and breed around the coasts of Antarctica. These flightless birds are well adapted to cold air and water, and scientists are concerned that they could be greatly affected by global warming. At the Antarctic Peninsula, average winter temperatures have increased by nearly 5°C in the last half-century, and the seas have also warmed up. This rise in temperature has had an effect on fish, krill and other sea creatures that penguins eat, resulting in a loss of food.

On small islands off Antarctica, researchers have found that since the mid-1970s the number of Adélie penguins has dropped from 32,000 breeding pairs to just 11,000. They have also discovered that the Adélies are being slowly replaced by Gentoo penguins. The Gentoos are migrating towards the South Pole from places such as the Falkland Islands, in search of colder waters and ice.

Wetlands

According to the Ramsar List of Wetlands of International Importance, the world's wetlands – including swamps, marshes, fens and bogs – cover an area of about 1.3 million square kilometres. That's an area 5 times the size of the United Kingdom. Wetlands are very important because of their biodiversity, but coastal wetlands are already being lost at a rate of up to 1.5 percent per year, due mainly to pollution and clearance for other uses, such as farming or housing. A rise in sea level will make this worse.

Coastal salt marshes and mangrove swamps could move slowly inland, but then they might meet human flood defences and farmland, which would lead to the wetlands dying out altogether. American scientists have calculated that a sea level rise of 0.3 metres could wipe out up to 43 percent of the USA's wetlands.

ESTIMATED REGIONAL AREA OF WETLANDS

The International Convention on Wetlands covers 150 countries and 1590 wetland sites.

region	million hectares	% of total
Africa	44.7	33
Central & South America	28.8	22
Europe	21.5	16
North America	19.6	15
Asia	11.3	8
Oceania	8.1	6
total	134.0	100

Source: Ramsar Convention on Wetlands/Wetlands International

According to the US National Resources Defense Council, sea level rise, increasing temperatures and alterations in rainfall will combine to damage the Everglades lake-marsh area in Florida. It has been estimated that the sea along the Florida coast is rising 6 to 10 times faster than the average rate for the region over the past 3,000 years. The Everglades area covers 6,100 square kilometres and supports a rich range of plants and animals. Because of the decline in their habitat, many birds of the Everglades region are already becoming rare, including the anhinga, or snakebird, which feeds on fish by spearing them with its long bill.

The Pantanal in Brazil is an amazing mixture of rivers, fresh water lakes, shrub-dominated wetlands, and seasonally flooded forests. It contains several endangered species, including hyacinth macaws, giant otters and marsh deer, as well as numerous nesting sites for the rare Jabiru stork. It also has 260 fish species. All this diversity of life is threatened by loss of such wetlands.

Mangrove forest covers the southern part of the USA's Everglades wetlands, where fresh water meets the salty sea. This makes an ideal environment for many plants and animals, but because it is low lying, the area is vulnerable to rising sea levels.

Forests and the carbon cycle

The world's rainforests play an important role in regulating the global climate. That is because trees are a major part of our planet's carbon cycle. All animals breathe carbon dioxide into the air. Plants, including trees, absorb this CO_2 to produce more food. This cycle keeps a natural balance of carbon dioxide and oxygen, as carbon moves to and from the Earth's atmosphere. As part of this process, forests, along with oceans, act as one of the planet's natural carbon sinks. They also assist the production of rainfall. Water evaporation is higher over forests than cleared land; the water turns to vapour and rises into the air, later forming clouds and producing rainfall.

The golden toad of Costa Rica is now extinct. Researchers believe that these toads were killed by a fungal disease, which was triggered by the changed climate of the cloud forest.

Over the last few decades, vast areas of forest have been cut down to clear the land for farming or urban development and to use the trees for timber. Much of the felled wood is burned as fuel, releasing carbon dioxide into the atmosphere. At the same time, cutting down forests reduces rainfall.

However, the causes of global warming are not so simple. Forests have a lower albedo (see page 10) than much-cleared land, so they keep the surface warmer. Also, scientists have recently discovered that forests give off more methane (see page 6) than was previously thought. Nevertheless, most scientists are convinced that deforestation contributes to global warming, while afforestation – turning land into forest – could help to limit it.

DEBATE

You are in charge
You belong to an environmental group that is creating a leaflet about deforestation and how it could affect the world's climate. What examples would you use to show how we could help to protect forests?

Moving up

As the world warms up, animals and plants that are adapted to cooler climates will try to move to higher latitudes or higher altitudes. Polar bears and penguins are examples of the former, as they move towards the North and South poles, respectively. Other animals and plants that live in the foothills or lower slopes of mountains will try to move higher up, though not all will be able to, because of the limits of the terrain. Cloud forest is evergreen mountainous forest, found in tropical areas, that has a low-level cloud cover. There is generally a small band of altitude – about 2,000 to 3,000 metres above sea level – that is just right for this environment of trees and plants. This kind of forest is being severely affected by global warming, as, in recent years, researchers have found an increase in clouds, but that they are forming at higher altitudes. This change is forcing plants to move higher up the mountain, where there is more cloud and it is cooler, but they will eventually run out of room.

The Monteverde cloud forest, in Costa Rica, is home to a variety of animals. These include howler and white-faced monkeys, snakes, frogs, moths and thousands of tropical birds, including 30 kinds of hummingbirds. In 1999 scientists reported that they thought the golden toad that previously lived in this forest was extinct.

CHAPTER 6

Weather Warnings

The García family have built up their small coffee-growing business in Santa Teresa, 1,500 metres up in the Peruvian Andes. Now, in 2020, they are benefiting from extra sales to tourists on the trail to the nearby Machu Picchu ancient Inca citadel. But the older members of the family live in constant fear of landslips and mudslides. They will always remember January 1998, when terrible El Niño rains swept away their small town, destroying many homes and killing 22 people. Since then there have been many more scares, and the warmer and wetter the summers become, the more fearful the family grow.

The likelihood of storms, drought and other extreme weather conditions increasing due to global warming is one of the great unknowns. Climatologists and other scientists are unsure about the future, and they do not all agree. However, it does seem that an increase in sea temperature will have an effect on ocean currents, the frequency of tropical storms and possibly some other hazardous weather phenomena, such as lake shrinkage and generally hotter, drier lands.

The El Niño effect

Since the early 1980s, a climate effect in the Pacific Ocean has become more frequent and more severe. The most famous part of the effect is known as El Niño (meaning 'boy child' in Spanish), because it usually begins around the time of the coming of the 'boy child', Jesus, at Christmas. El Niño happens when the normal easterly trade winds weaken or even reverse direction. This causes the upper layer of warm water in the western Pacific to flow eastwards towards the upper part of South

A stream of trucks help survivors of the 1998 El Niño mudslide in Peru make their way downhill with any possessions they can recover.

America. The climate changes of El Niño cause increased rainfall and storms along the west coast of North and South America, and at the other extreme, drought in Indonesia and Australia.

A strong El Niño typically occurs every three to seven years, and it may last for up to a year. Scientists often refer to it as ENSO (for El Niño–Southern Oscillation). The oscillation refers to the change between El Niño, normal conditions and a third phenomenon called La Niña ('girl child'). During La Niña, warm surface water flows towards Asia, leaving colder deep-sea water to come to the surface near the Americas. The chart below shows how sea surface temperatures have changed in the eastern Pacific Ocean at the beginning of this century, starting with a period of La Niña that was followed by an El Niño episode.

The strongest El Niño conditions on record were in 1997–98. They caused torrential rains, floods and mudslides in Peru, as well as violent storms in California. There were also ferocious forest fires in Indonesia because of the intensely dry conditions.

SEA SURFACE TEMPERATURE CHANGE

Scientists use a threshold of 0.5°C above or below normal sea temperature to determine El Niño and La Niña conditions. They usually call a period of 5 consecutive months above the threshold an El Niño episode, and 5 months below, a La Niña episode.

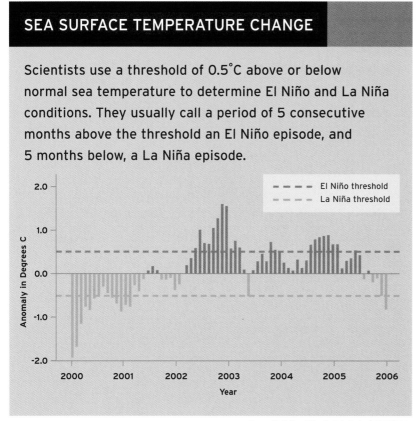

Source: US National Climatic Data Center/NESDIS/NOAA

Ocean currents

The circulation of ocean currents acts like a giant conveyor belt, moving warm and cold water around the planet. The currents are driven by differences in water temperature and salinity (level of saltiness), and so could be altered by global warming. The Gulf Stream is a major current that takes warm water from the tropical Caribbean Sea up into the North Atlantic Ocean towards northern Europe. Westerly winds are also warmed as they cross the Gulf Stream, and they help give Western Europe milder winters than other regions of the same latitude.

There are concerns that global warming could weaken the Gulf Stream, which depends on cool water sinking in the north and travelling back south, where it warms again, rises and heads north. As the Arctic ice melts (see Chapter 2), the fresh water would make the ocean less salty, and therefore less dense so that it does not sink. The circulation would be weakened. Studies have shown that the Gulf Stream slowed by nearly one-third in the 12 years up until 2005. If this trend continues, it is expected to have a major effect on European climate, leading to colder winters, more frequent storms and severe weather.

DEBATE

You are in charge
You work for the UN World Meteorological Organization and are given the opportunity on a radio programme to say briefly how climate research can help highlight the potential effects of global warming. What are the main points to put across?

Deserts and droughts

The world's deserts – defined as dry regions that receive less than 25 centimetres of rain a year – cover about one-fifth of the Earth's land area. Scientists are uncertain about what the consequences of global warming will be on deserts. Some predict more rainfall and, therefore, more clouds and lower temperatures. Others are more worried about the problem of desertification – the process by which dry regions grow bigger, spread and become deserts. This process is at least partly caused by global warming. In 1994 the United Nations set up a Convention to Combat Desertification (UNCCD), and its researchers believe that growing desertification affects one-third of the Earth's surface and the lives of more than 1 billion people.

About one-third of the world's dry lands are in Africa, with another third in Asia, and the rest spread around the other continents. Chad is in an African region known as the Sahel, which lies just to the south of the Sahara Desert. Here, global warming is making the land drier (see page 25). Along with other factors, such as the increase in human and livestock population and poor land management, global warming is adding to the problems of desertification.

A US Forest Service helicopter deliberately starts a fire to clear the ground and stop an advancing wildfire in California. More heat means more forest fires, and hot, dry regions such as this are most at risk.

CHAPTER 7

Fuel for Transport

There is record attendance at the 2020 International Motor Show in Geneva. This annual event has been famous since 1905 for introducing all the latest designs, prototypes and concept cars. But things are different now. Instead of looking for fast new supercars or powerful four-wheel drives, buyers are searching for innovation in the use of fuel. They still want stylish vehicles with plenty of comfort and safety features, but more than anything else, they want to please ordinary motorists and avoid heavy taxes by offering vehicles that are both economical and environmentally friendly. Petrol-driven engines are rare compared to the latest fuel-cell models.

Transport is a major user of energy and a big contributor to greenhouse gas emissions. More than one-fifth of the world's energy is used in transport by being turned into motor power. The other large energy users are industry and buildings, with a smaller proportion used in agriculture. Scientists have calculated that in the early 21st century about 30 percent of greenhouse gas emissions come from transport. This is because most vehicles burn fossil fuels.

A motorist fills up with petrol, which will give off exhaust gases as it burns.

Today's fuels

For many years the main fuels for transport have been petrol, diesel oil and kerosene (paraffin oil). They are all made from the same raw material – crude oil – and more than one-third of the world's oil is refined into petrol. Every day we burn nearly 3 billion litres of petrol, mostly in cars; more than two-fifths of petrol is used in the United States. Diesel oil needs less refining and is used by some cars, lorries and buses, as well as by railway locomotives and ships. Jet aircraft burn kerosene.

Difficulties in predicting the future

Experts try to predict how much carbon dioxide and other greenhouse gases we will release into the atmosphere in the future. Of course, they don't know and can only make an educated guess. The Intergovernmental Panel on Climate Change uses many different future scenarios, including the number of cars on the roads and possible changes in industrial processes, to forecast the future, including possible CO_2 emissions. In their figures, the number of gigatonnes (or billions of tonnes) of emissions in 2020 varies between a low of 8 and a possible high of 13. They say that by 2050 the figure could still be as low as 9 (or 10, as shown in the table), but it could be as high as 23 gigatonnes if we do not change to using other fuels.

FOSSIL FUELS AND TRANSPORT 1990-2050

The scientists who produced these predictions used average figures, based on how they think people all over the world might use fossil fuels.

Percentage of transport fuel from fossil fuels

1990	2000	2010	2020	2030	2040	2050
97	91	81	74	63	57	52

Emissions from fossil fuels in gigatonnes of carbon

1990	2000	2010	2020	2030	2040	2050
5.8	6.9	8.0	9.2	10.7	10.6	10.0

Source: International Energy Agency/ International Institute for Applied Systems Analysis

Air travel

Air travel presents a special problem in terms of greenhouse gas emission. Aircraft emit gases and particles high in the atmosphere, and these are thought to be particularly damaging, especially to the ozone layer. It has been estimated that aircraft contribute about 3 percent of the CO_2 that comes from human sources. They also emit water vapour, a greenhouse gas, which we sometimes see as vapour trails in the sky. The vapour increases high cloud cover, which also has a blanketing effect on the Earth's surface.

Since the beginning of the 1990s, air travel has been increasing by more than 5 percent every year. There are more aircraft, more airports, more flights and more passengers. The growth figures shown in the chart below are calculated in passenger-kilometres – the number of passengers multiplied by the distance they fly. In 2005 the total number of passengers for the year reached 4 billion, a 6 percent increase from the previous year.

Trades, taxes and offsets

Some people feel that airlines should pay for the damage they cause to the atmosphere and their considerable contribution to the greenhouse effect and global warming. One way to achieve this is to include airlines in an emissions trading scheme. The total amount of

SCHEDULED PASSENGER TRAFFIC IN BILLIONS OF PASSENGER-KILOMETRES

Area	1993	2005	% increase
Africa	43.3	73.1	+ 68.8%
Asia/Pacific	440.1	879.6	+ 99.9%
Europe	498.1	911.9	+ 83.1%
Middle East	58.4	134.0	+ 129.5%
North America	813.8	1199.3	+ 47.4%
Latin America/Caribbean	95.7	149.5	+ 74.4%
WORLD	1949.4	3347.4	+ 71.7%

Source: International Civil Aviation Organization

emissions would be agreed, and airlines could buy allowances in the form of permits to emit CO_2. The permits could be bought and sold to meet emission reduction targets.

Another way to make airlines pay for their emissions is to increase taxes on aviation. Ultimately, both of these schemes would lead to an increase in ticket prices, as the airlines passed on the costs to their customers. Alternatively, passengers could enter an offset scheme. Offset schemes – which give people the opportunity to pay for the carbon emissions that they cause – have already been established. The money raised is used to fund projects that aim to combat the further enhancement of the greenhouse effect. There are projects to improve energy efficiency (reducing the amount of fuel needed) and provide renewable energy (reducing the use of fossil fuels).

If you flew to Geneva for the Motor Show, for example, you could calculate how much CO_2 you would need to offset. This could be converted into a payment, which would be invested into a fund. One passenger's return flight to Geneva from London creates an emission of 0.17 tonnes of CO_2; from New York it would be 1.74 tonnes, and from Tokyo 2.74 tonnes. In 2006 the offset cost for the longest (Tokyo) flight would be £21 – not a lot of money on top of the fare.

Aircraft parked at Charles de Gaulle airport, Paris, which handled nearly 54 million passengers in 2005. The world's busiest airport was Atlanta, Georgia, USA, with nearly 86 million passengers. Increased air traffic will add to greenhouse gas emissions.

On the road

Cars are more popular than ever, and the vast majority run on petrol or diesel. These all give off CO_2, but there is a great difference between various models. A small city car, for example, emits 113 grams of CO_2 per kilometre and travels 21 kilometres on every litre of fuel. A large sports car, on the other hand, emits 394 g/km and does just 6 km/l. In the UK and many other countries, regulations have been brought

Buses and trams compete with cars in Hong Kong. Good public transport is vital in modern cities, with integrated systems linking road travel with overland and underground trains. If the system is efficient, more people will be able to leave their cars at home.

in so that road taxes are higher for drivers of cars that produce more pollution. When you consider that at least 44 million cars are manufactured throughout the world every year, it is clearly important to reduce the amount of CO_2 that they emit.

Biofuels and hybrids

One way to replace fossil fuels is to run cars on fuel from biomass, an energy source that includes all plant matter and animal waste, which also produces usable gases in landfill sites and sewage plants. The carbon dioxide released by burning biomass is no greater than the amount that was taken in by the growing plants. Also, carbon dioxide will be absorbed by plants that grow in place of the harvested crop. This is called a closed carbon cycle and makes biomass a carbon-neutral resource – it does not increase the overall amount of CO_2 in the atmosphere, except by its associated transport emissions. In Brazil, sugar cane is used as a source of fuel, and most new Brazilian cars are capable of running on pure ethanol (also called E-100). Ethanol can also be made from other grasses such as maize and barley, or from plants such as sugar beet or potatoes. Pure or blended biodiesel can be produced by extracting oil from soybeans, rapeseed or peanuts. Another option is the hybrid car, which combines a petrol, diesel or biofuel engine with an electric motor that takes over at low speeds. The battery for the electric motor is recharged by the action of the brakes. Honda, Toyota and other car manufacturers are increasing their sales of hybrids.

Fuel cells

Hydrogen gas is a very useful carrier of energy, and it can be used as a fuel to generate electricity and power cars. Hydrogen fuel cells convert chemical energy to electrical energy by combining hydrogen and oxygen. There is a drawback: the energy needed to make the hydrogen is often from a fossil fuel and emits CO_2. However, the hydrogen could be made from water using electricity generated from renewable sources.

DEBATE

You are in charge
You work for an international travel company that has to put up its prices to pay for higher air costs and carbon taxes. How would you explain the increases to customers?

CHAPTER 8

What Can We Do?

It is September 2020 and members of an environmental group are meeting at an eco-village. The residents of the village use solar panels and wind turbines to create their own energy, and they recycle everything that they can. But they and their guests know that lifestyle changes will not be enough to limit climate change due to global warming during the rest of the 21st century. They discuss other ways to slow down and stabilize climate change and draw up an action plan to convince politicians that new agreements are needed. The Tokyo meeting in March this year was a start, but these environmentalists believe that more action is urgently needed.

One of the most obvious ways in which we can avoid making the situation worse is to stop pumping so much carbon dioxide into the Earth's atmosphere. This is not easy when experts say that the demand for electricity, for example, will nearly double by 2030. Currently, about one-third of primary energy goes to generate electricity, most of which is produced by burning fossil fuels. Yet we could use renewable sources to satisfy more of our energy needs, and there are promising developments in the use of hydro, biomass, solar, wind, geothermal, tidal and wave power.

Energy mix

Some experts think that renewable sources will never be enough and that without fossil fuels we could be left with an 'energy gap'. There is

PROJECTED USE OF RENEWABLE ENERGY

	year 1990 %	year 2020 %
traditional biomass (woodfuels, etc.)	10.6	9.3
hydro (water)	5.3	5.8
modern biomass (biofuels, waste, etc.)	1.4	5.0
solar	0.1	3.1
wind	0.0	1.9
geothermal (Earth's heat)	0.1	0.8
micro-hydro (small water generators)	0.2	0.6
tidal and wave	0.0	0.5
TOTAL	17.7	27.0

Source: World Energy Council

another alternative – nuclear power. This is not a renewable resource, because nuclear fuel (from the mined radioactive metal uranium) is used up to produce power. But one of the big advantages of nuclear power is that it produces a huge amount of energy from a small amount of fuel. Another advantage that is very important when considering global warming is that nuclear processes do not release carbon dioxide. Yet there are big disadvantages, too, including the problems of nuclear waste and possible accidents at nuclear power stations. Other worries are the link with nuclear weapons and the possibility that terrorists might obtain nuclear material and use it for the wrong purpose.

The many and varied advantages and disadvantages of different energy sources lead many to believe that we should be looking for a good mix, rather than to totally exclude any one of them.

Small and self-sufficient

Another way forward is to use more micro-systems, in which individual homes or communities have their own wind turbine, solar panels or water turbine. In many countries there are schemes to help people with the costs of installing these micro-generators. In Spain, for example, there is now a requirement to build solar panels into the roofs of all new homes.

This energy-efficient house in California has a turf roof for insulation and solar panels to provide electricity.

You can still be connected to the national electricity grid in case your micro-generator does not consistently provide enough energy. There is another incentive, too. If your micro-system is so successful that it produces more electricity than your household or community needs, you can sell any surplus electricity to the national grid to be used by others.

International agreements

By the terms of the Kyoto Protocol (see page 4), the developed and industrialized countries of the world agreed to reduce their emissions of greenhouse gases by at least 5.2 percent of their 1990 levels, by the year 2012. That's a reduction of about 29 percent on the emissions that would otherwise be expected by then. According to the UN, reductions of only 3.5 percent had been made by early 2006.

One problem with this international agreement is that it has not been ratified by Australia or by the world's biggest emitter of CO_2, the United States. The USA produced 5,838 million tonnes of CO_2 in

A demonstrator shows his support for the UN Climate Change Conference in Montréal, Canada, in 2005. Conference delegates looked ahead to what their countries could do to limit global warming after 2012.

2002 – that's almost one-quarter of the world's total, while Australia produced 356 million tonnes.

The top five emitters of CO_2 are the USA (24.3%), China (14.5%), Russia (5.9%), India (5.1%) and Japan (5.0%). The Kyoto agreement classifies both China and India as developing countries, which means that they are not required to make reductions by 2012. However, both of these countries have rapidly growing economies and vast populations, and are therefore committed to much greater energy production and use. It is therefore likely that the international community will want to change China and India's classification when they agree what is to happen by 2020.

The governments of some countries, particularly the USA, are concerned that a reduction in energy use will harm their economy and worsen unemployment. They are also worried that less use of fossil fuels will leave them with an 'energy gap' that renewable sources cannot fill. But experts say that renewable sources could be much more efficient than they currently are, if more research and development were put into them now.

Individual responsibility

Although as individuals we cannot stop the polar ice caps from melting, or the seas from rising, we can all help in our own way to reduce greenhouse gas emissions and make a valuable contribution to limiting global warming. We can use energy more wisely and efficiently, such as switching off lights when we leave the room and not leaving electrical appliances on standby. We can also travel more sensibly, sharing cars so that we save fuel, using public transport and energy-efficient vehicles (see pages 40–41), and especially by walking or cycling whenever possible.

DEBATE

You are in charge
You are a government minister looking into the use of energy resources. Which of these sources would you choose to prioritize:

- fossil fuels (oil, gas, coal)
- nuclear energy
- renewable sources (biomass, solar, wind, geothermal, hydro)?

All the measures that are being taken by international communities and individuals can make a difference to global warming. If we were to do nothing, the situation would undoubtedly be more difficult by 2020. That would leave the responsibility – and the problems – to future generations. We must all take responsibility now.

Glossary

afforestation The conversion of land into forest by planting new trees.

albedo effect The capacity of a surface to reflect the Sun's warmth and light. Snow and ice have a high albedo; brown earth has a low albedo.

atoll A ring-shaped series of coral islands surrounding a shallow lagoon.

biodiversity The variety of plant and animal life in the world or in a particular habitat or region.

biofuel A fuel produced from biomass.

biomass All plant and animal matter.

carbon cycle The series of interlinked processes on Earth by which carbon compounds are exchanged between living things and the atmosphere.

climate The general weather conditions in an area over a long period of time.

climatologist A scientist who studies climate.

coelenterate An animal in a family of sea animals that includes corals, jellyfishes and sea anemones.

deficit The amount by which something is too small (such as production compared with consumption).

deforestation The cutting down and removal of forest trees.

delta The area near the mouth of some rivers, where the flow splits into several different channels.

desertification The process by which fertile dry land becomes desert.

ecosystem A group of living things that are dependent on each other and their environment.

El Niño Periodic changes in winds and currents of the Pacific Ocean that bring extreme weather to countries around the ocean; see also ENSO.

emission The process of emitting, or producing and giving off, something such as a gas.

ENSO (El Niño–Southern Oscillation) The cycle of changes between El Niño, normal and La Niña conditions in the Pacific region.

environmentalist A person who is concerned about and acts to protect the natural environment.

fossil fuel A fuel (such as coal, oil and natural gas) that comes from the fossilized remains of prehistoric plants and animals; fossil fuels are non-renewable.

geothermal The heat from within the Earth.

glacier A slowly-moving mass or river of ice formed by compacted snow on high ground.

greenhouse effect The warming of the Earth's surface by the natural effect of a blanket of certain gases in the atmosphere. The effect is increased by gases such as carbon dioxide emitted by human activity, especially from burning fossil fuels.

greenhouse gas A gas, such as carbon dioxide, that traps heat from the Sun near the Earth and helps create the greenhouse effect.

groundwater Water held underground in porous rocks.

hydroelectricity Electricity generated by moving water, especially from a dam across a river.

ice age Any of the periods in history when there were ice sheets across large parts of the Earth's surface.

ice cap A covering of ice over a large area.

ice sheet A thick layer of ice over a large area that remains frozen for a long period.

ice shelf A floating sheet of ice that is attached to coastal land.

indigenous people The original or native people of a region.

interglacial period A period between ice ages.

irrigate To water land in order to help crops to grow.

La Niña Changes in the Pacific Ocean that bring cold water to the surface; see also ENSO.

levee An embankment built to stop flooding.

meteorologist A scientist who studies and forecasts the weather.

ozone layer A layer of ozone gas high in the Earth's atmosphere that absorbs most ultraviolet radiation from the Sun.

pack ice A mass of ice floating on the sea.

parasite An animal that lives on or in another host organism.

permafrost Ground in the polar regions that remains permanently frozen.

polder An area of land reclaimed from the sea and protected by embankments.

pollute To damage (the environment, atmosphere, etc.) with harmful substances.

primary energy The energy available in a natural energy source (such as coal or sunlight) before it is changed into motor power or electricity. Some of the primary energy is wasted during the change to another form of power.

protocol A formal agreement between nations.

ratify To approve something formally so that it comes into effect.

renewable energy A source of energy that does not run out by being used, such as water, wind, solar or geothermal power; the term includes sources that can be replaced, such as biomass.

summit A meeting between heads of government to discuss important international matters.

tsunami Huge destructive waves caused by an undersea earthquake.

wetland Land, such as marshes or swamps, that is saturated or covered with water for most of the time.

wildfire A fierce fire that spreads rapidly, especially a forest fire.

Further Information

Books

Climate Change: Our impact on the Planet by Simon Scoones (Hodder Wayland, 2004)

Global Warming: A Beginner's Guide to our Changing Climate by Fred Pearce (Dorling Kindersley, 2002)

Global Warming: A Very Short Introduction by Mark Maslin (Oxford University Press, 2004)

Websites

www.climateprediction.net or **www.bbc.co.uk/climatechange**
You could use your computer to join in the largest climate prediction experiment ever, developed by climatologists using the Meteorological Office climate model.

www.greenpeace.org.uk/climate
Interesting practical information from the global environmental organization, which looks for solutions and alternatives. Greenpeace campaigns for the "phasing-out of fossil fuels and the promotion of renewable energies in order to stop climate change".

www.ipcc.ch
The Intergovernmental Panel on Climate Change assesses all information concerning "the scientific basis of risk of human-induced climate change". A very informative website with the latest technical information and statistics.

http://news.bbc.co.uk/1/hi/in_depth/ sci_tech/2004/climate_change
The BBC guide to climate change, including features, analysis, background, in-depth reports and news stories, as well as a good set of links to other websites.

http://yosemite.epa.gov/oar/ globalwarming.nsf/content/index.html
Information on global warming from the US Environmental Protection Agency, including a section on "Individuals can make a difference".

Debate Panel answers

Page 7:
All five measures are important, so it is difficult to put them in order of priority. Most experts think that the first thing to put right is to reduce CO_2 emissions, and all the actions would help this.

Page 13:
You could concentrate on how the changing environment will affect local people's lives. You might want to focus on ways in which a traditional way of life can be combined with modern progress. You could use figures from these pages or more local statistics for your community (perhaps from the Arctic Council). The Arctic Council concentrates on environmental, social and economic issues.

Page 18:
You might argue that all nations should be accountable, but that the biggest emitters of CO_2 – the USA and the European Union as a group – should pay most to help those who cannot afford to help themselves.

Page 25:
You could reply that many scientists believe that global warming will lead to big changes in water supplies, including rivers. However, the situation is complicated by many other factors, such as land management. Your local scientists, engineers and politicians will need to take all these into consideration when reviewing plans for the dam.

Page 31:
Here are just some examples. Governments and politicians could monitor logging more closely and prosecute illegal loggers. Publishers could use recycled and so-called forest-friendly paper for their books (many do this already, but not all). We can all look carefully at the wood (such as furniture) that we buy; it should be certified by the Forest Stewardship Council (FSC).

Page 34:
The WMO conducts climate research that, it says, provides vital information for advance warnings that save lives and reduce damage to property and the environment. You could quote this and use the ability to predict such events as droughts or El Niños as possible examples.

Page 41:
You could mention the concerns about the greenhouse effect and global warming. You could also encourage your company to produce an explanatory leaflet, which has the advantage of showing that it cares for the environment as well as its customers.

Page 45:
Some countries have an energy policy based on all available energy sources. To limit greenhouse gases, renewable sources are best. Some countries, such as France, favour nuclear power stations, but these present huge problems such as radioactive waste disposal. Fossil fuels are worst for global warming and will not last forever. You might suggest a mix with the priority on renewable sources.

Index

Page numbers in **bold** refer to illustrations.

Early Sea Painters

1660-1730

Frontispiece. L.d. Man. *Magnified view of part of the rigging of the* Royal Sovereign *(Colour Plate 34) showing the typical careful drawing of the numerous small figures all doing something appropriate and all wearing little hats!*

Early Sea Painters

1660–1730

The group who worked in England
under the shadow of the Van de Veldes

F.B. Cockett

ANTIQUE COLLECTORS' CLUB

© 1995 F.B. Cockett
World copyright reserved

ISBN 1 85149 230 5

The right of F.B. Cockett to be identified as author of this work
has been asserted by him in accordance with
the Copyright, Designs and Patents Act 1988

British Library Cataloguing-in-Publication Data
A catalogue record for this book is available from the British Library

Printed in England
by the Antique Collectors' Club Ltd., Woodbridge, Suffolk
on Consort Royal Satin paper
supplied by the Donside Paper Company, Aberdeen, Scotland

L.d. Man. *Magnified view of the stern of the* Royal Sovereign *(Colour Plate 34) to show the detailed and lovingly rendered stern decoration.* Private Collection

*To Dorothea, my wife, who
helped me along the way, and
got deeply involved with all this.*

THE ANTIQUE COLLECTORS' CLUB

The Antique Collectors' Club was formed in 1966 and quickly grew to a five figure membership spread throughout the world. It publishes the only independently run monthly antiques magazine, *Antique Collecting*, which caters for those collectors who are interested in widening their knowledge of antiques, both by greater awareness of quality and by discussion of the factors which influence the price that is likely to be asked. The Antique Collectors' Club pioneered the provision of information on prices for collectors and the magazine still leads in the provision of detailed articles on a variety of subjects.

It was in response to the enormous demand for information on 'what to pay' that the price guide series was introduced in 1968 with the first edition of *The Price Guide to Antique Furniture* (completely revised 1978 and 1989), a book which broke new ground by illustrating the more common types of antique furniture, the sort that collectors could buy in shops and at auctions rather than the rare museum pieces which had previously been used (and still to a large extent are used) to make up the limited amount of illustrations in books published by commercial publishers. Many other price guides have followed, all copiously illustrated, and greatly appreciated by collectors for the valuable information they contain, quite apart from prices. The Price Guide Series heralded the publication of many standard works of reference on art and antiques. *The Dictionary of British Art* (now in six volumes), *The Pictorial Dictionary of British 19th Century Furniture Design, Oak Furniture* and *Early English Clocks* were followed by many deeply researched reference works such as *The Directory of Gold and Silversmiths,* providing new information. Many of these books are now accepted as the standard work of reference on their subject.

The Antique Collectors' Club has widened its list to include books on gardens and architecture. All the Club's publications are available through bookshops world wide and a full catalogue of all these titles is available free of charge from the addresses below.

Club membership, open to all collectors, costs little. Members receive free of charge *Antique Collecting*, the Club's magazine (published ten times a year), which contains well-illustrated articles dealing with the practical aspects of collecting not normally dealt with by magazines. Prices, features of value, investment potential, fakes and forgeries are all given prominence in the magazine.

Among other facilities available to members are private buying and selling facilities, the longest list of 'For Sales' of any antiques magazine, an annual ceramics conference and the opportunity to meet other collectors at their local antique collectors' clubs. There are over eighty in Britain and more than a dozen overseas. Members may also buy the Club's publications at special pre-publication prices.

As its motto implies, the Club is an organisation designed to help collectors get the most out of their hobby: it is informal and friendly and gives enormous enjoyment to all concerned.

For Collectors — By Collectors — About Collecting

ANTIQUE COLLECTORS' CLUB
5 Church Street, Woodbridge Suffolk IP12 1DS, UK
Tel: 01394 385501 Fax: 01394 384434
—— or ——
Market Street Industrial Park, Wappingers' Falls, NY 12590, USA
Tel: 914 297 0003 Fax: 914 297 0068

Colour Plate 1. *The Spanish Armada. Painted by an English artist (probably Nicholas Hilliard), c.1590. It is the first attempt by a native English artist at a 'seascape'. Canvas. 48in. x 112in. Painted in celebration of the defeat of the Armada, this picture provides a loose summary of several aspects of the event, rather than attempting a literal representation of fact. It amalgamates a number of locations and occurrences into one imaginative scene: Elizabeth's address to her troops at Tilbury is portrayed on the left; the action offshore refers to several phases in the battle; and the English coastline is represented with beacons, but given an exotic Mediterranean flavour (characteristic of earlier 16th century Flemish painting). The galleon on the right flying the royal standard seems intended to be the Ark Royal, but the Spanish ships to her left are not identifiable. The absence of certain necessary spars, rigging and sails suggests that the artist was not a marine painter by training. A traditional attribution to Nicholas Hilliard — on the basis of a report that an Armada subject by Hilliard had been in Charles I's collection — is intriguing.* SOCIETY OF APOTHECARIES, LONDON

CONTENTS

(N.M.M. = National Maritime Museum, Greenwich)

ACKNOWLEDGEMENTS

It is a pleasure to acknowledge the continuing help and encouragement given to me by the National Maritime Museum, Greenwich. In particular Mr. M.S. Robinson, Mr. David Cordingley and Mr. Roger Quarm have been very patient and unfailingly helpful, as have all the members of the departments of painting and drawing.

I must also record my debt to Mr. E.H.H. Archibald's book, *The Dictionary of Sea Painters,* and to his lectures on the Van de Veldes and the early sea painters of Britain. Mr. Robinson's great two volume work of reference on the Van de Veldes has been a continuous source of essential information. The Witt Library, where I have spent many hours, has been extremely co-operative, as has also the Dulwich Picture Gallery. Her Majesty, Queen Elizabeth, has lent a photograph of an important very early seascape from the Royal Collection.

I must also add my thanks to the picture departments of the four main salerooms of London – Christie's, Sotheby's, Bonhams and Phillips – for their kindness and patience. Mr. Thomas Ward of Bonhams has taken many of the photographs in this book.

Picture dealers, such as O'Mell, Leger Galleries, the Parker Gallery, the Rutland Gallery, Lowndes Lodge Gallery and Raphael Valls have been very helpful.

My thanks also to my daughter Mrs. Judith Aldrick for access to her original research on Isaac Sailmaker, which she did during her period at the National Maritime Museum, and to Mrs. Doris Toms who has struggled successfully with my almost illegible script to produce a beautifully typed manuscript.

Finally, I must thank my wife, Dorothea, for her continued interest and help at all stages of production of this work, including many of the photographs taken at awkward times and in difficult places over many years. Her critical interest in the pictures has been a great and helpful stimulus at all times.

L.d. Man. *Portrait of the Royal Sovereign of 1701.*   PRIVATE COLLECTION

INTRODUCTION

In 1966 I bought a painting of a large eighteenth century warship – said to be of the *Royal Sovereign* of 1701. It had been on exhibition at the Rye Art Gallery in a small marine painting exhibition. It was attributed to Peter Monamy and was a most attractive and very detailed early ship portrait (Colour Plate 34 and above).

At lower left it had what I thought was the remains of a signature which looked like P. Mon. Luckily, I was able to show it to Mr. Michael Robinson of the National Maritime Museum. He pointed out that the signature was actually that of L. d. Man, a virtually unknown early marine artist. Certainly, I could find no reference to him except, finally, in an obscure file at the National Maritime Museum.

This was my introduction to a fascinating group of early marine painters working in England roughly between 1660 and 1730, about whom relatively little was known.

Looking back at the history of painting in England, up to the end of the fifteenth century it hardly existed at all. Henry VIII at the beginning of the sixteenth century had to import Holbein for his portraits, but even so the most basic subjects were extremely thin on the ground. During the second half of the sixteenth century and early years of the seventeenth century, covered by the reigns of Elizabeth I and James I, portrait painting became a fashionable art. Several Flemish and French painters visited England, but in addition a small group of rather primitive 'home grown' painters made their appearance, such as Nicholas Hilliard, George Gower, William Larkin and Robert Peake. Most of them confined their efforts to portraits, although in response to great historical occasions, such as the defeat of the Spanish Armada in 1588, one of them, probably Nicholas Hilliard, produced a large rather primitive historical narrative painting of the event. This painting (Colour Plate 1) is owned by the Society of Apothecaries, London, and probably represents the first major attempt at a maritime subject by an English artist.

There is one other early 'seascape' painted during the reign of Henry VIII soon after 1520, and now in the Royal Collection at Hampton Court Palace (see Plate 47). This shows the departure of Henry VIII from Dover for his meeting with Francis I of France at the Field of the Cloth of Gold. It is by an unknown artist, probably Flemish, and shows a fleet of early English ships assembled off Dover (including Henry's biggest ship, the *Great Harry).*

One of the most extraordinary things about art history of the fifteenth and sixteenth centuries is that all the European powers of the period (especially Spain and Portugal) had large and colourful fleets of galleys and caravels and galleons, yet no artists emerged who made it their business to paint and illustrate these ships. Art was almost exclusively religious, allegorical and portraiture. Certainly marine painting did not exist as a serious art form, particularly in England.

Thus when the Earl of Nottingham in the 1590s wished to have the defeat of the Spanish Armada commemorated, he had to commission the early Dutch marine painter Hendrick Cornelius Vroom (1566-1640) to make the cartoons for the famous Armada tapestries which were hung in the Palace of Westminster. Engravings were made from these, which are still in existence and can be seen at the National Maritime Museum, Greenwich. The original tapestries were destroyed by fire in 1834.

By the time Charles I came to the throne in 1625 serious interest in painting started to revive as he imported Van Dyck who inspired a new and more sophisticated style of portraiture.

Marine painting, however, had to wait until Charles II appeared (1660-1685). Charles and his brother James (later James II) spent the years 1649 to 1660 in exile in the 'low countries' (now Holland and Belgium). At that time Holland was the pre-eminent naval power and had enormous fleets of warships and trading vessels and fishing vessels of all sorts. The great seventeenth century

School of Dutch painting was flourishing, and a school of painters grew up who specialised in recording all the marine activity. Charles and his brother grew to love ships and the sea and also admired the work of the Dutch painters.

When Charles was recalled to the throne in 1660 he was able to gratify his love of sailing. The Dutch gave him a yacht as a leaving present (as it were) and he very soon had a small fleet of yachts – small, fast, sea-worthy and easily handled vessels, which were also beautiful to look at – in which he and his brother sailed *for pleasure*. This was indeed quite a new activity for an English King, and it astonished many of his subjects (including Pepys).

However, he soon began to notice the complete lack of artistic talent in England which allowed all this marine activity, and the truly magnificent ships of the period, to go unrecorded. As a result, in 1672 he issued a proclamation inviting Dutch artists to come and live and work in England. This was during the third Dutch War which was going badly for Holland. The Dutch economy was in severe distress, and the market for luxuries, such as pictures, was drying up. So, during the next few years, many of them took advantage of this invitation, and a small flood of very good artists migrated to London. Amongst them were the two acknowledged best marine artists of the day, the Van de Veldes.

The main outline of the evolution of marine painting in England is well known. It began with the arrival of the Van de Veldes (father and son) from Holland in 1673. They came at the invitation of Charles II and occupied a studio in the Queen's House at Greenwich. Both of them were already mature and talented artists, trained in the great mid-seventeenth century school of Dutch marine painting. They established a studio of British marine painting which catered for the King and his court, the aristocracy and the emerging

Adrian van Diest. *This is one of his typical long narrow harbour capriccio scenes, designed for an 'over-door' or 'over-window' situation.*
CHRISTIE'S

Jacob Knyff. *An English two-decker and a Dutch flagship off Dover.*   PRIVATE COLLECTION

well-to-do English merchants and professional classes. The demand became so great that the original studio expanded and during its later years· (roughly 1690-1707) it became a 'picture factory' with an enormous output, employing at least two and probably more studio assistants. During this period the two main studio assistants that are known for certain were Cornelis van de Velde (William van de Velde the Younger's son) and Johan van der Hagen.

Cornelis van de Velde carried on the studio, with the help of his assistants, for several years after Van de Velde the Younger's death in 1707.

There is no other pre-eminent name in British marine painting until Peter Monamy begins to emerge in the 1730s as the most well-known and successful English practitioner. He is followed closely by a number of well-known names, such as Francis Swaine, Samuel Scott, John Clevely, Charles Brooking and Dominic Serres. These artists between them covered the marine scene of the mid-eighteenth century as a flourishing and very competent 'British School'.

The Van de Veldes so dominated the world of marine painting, even in their own life time, that the existence of a number of other attractive and competent marine artists working in England between 1660 and 1730 received little attention. These men became the subject of my own special interest over the last thirty years. Unfortunately, documentary evidence about them is almost totally lacking, and resurgence of knowledge about them is based largely on comparative study of pictures emerging from salerooms, in museum collections and in private collections throughout this country and in Europe.

This relatively unknown group includes Isaac Sailmaker, Jacob Knyff, J.K.D. van Beecq, Adrian van Diest, L. Castro, L. d. Man. and H. and R. Vale. In addition to these people the men from the tail-end of the Van de Velde studio – namely Cornelis van de Velde and J. van der Hagen – were also producing pictures.

The search for pictures and scraps of knowledge about these painters was a fascinating exercise over the years, and they gradually emerged as considerable personalities in their own right.

Most of them were fine artists, with an individuality of their own, producing attractive and historically interesting and important pictures. They have been appearing in British salerooms with increasing frequency in the last ten years or so, and it is a tribute to them that their works are increasingly sought by collectors, with the inevitable rise in prices paid for them. The purpose of this little book is to fill in the gap in knowledge about marine painting between the Van de Veldes and Peter Monamy, which roughly spans the years 1675 to 1730.

One of the main difficulties about the recognition of some of these painters is the lack of signatures on their works. It is not until quite a large body of their pictures has been seen that certain characteristics become recognisable. Some hardly ever signed their work (like Sailmaker and J. Knyff). With most of the others, small numbers of signed works are available to give a lead. In others, the signature may have been removed, either intentionally as in some Brookings (see page 119), or unintentionally by over cleaning.

The situation is further complicated by the number of artists who began their artistic career by making copies of Van de Velde subjects. Excellent Van de Velde copies, or slightly altered versions of Van de Veldes, were made by Peter Monamy, Dominic Serres, R. Woodcock and Adrian van Diest. Sometimes they were signed, sometimes not. Some were undoubtedly sold as genuine Van de Veldes. The buying public were so brain washed as to what a 'Marine Picture' should be like that they still wanted 'Van de Veldes' even some time after his death in 1707.

It is probable that the two Van de Velde studio assistants, Cornelis van de Velde and J. van der Hagen continued to provide 'Van de Veldes' for this market for several years after 1707. This was quite understandable as they had probably done most of the painting on the many marine pictures coming out of the studio for the last years while Van de Velde was still alive. (Mr. M.S. Robinson's monumental work on the Van de Veldes should be consulted by those interested in this aspect.)

The illustrations in this book aim to demonstrate the range of the painter under discussion, as well as the characteristics of his techniques. Important and major pictures tend to become better known from repeated photographs in various books and journals. Smaller more routine or 'run of the mill' pictures, although often no less charming than the major ones, do not receive so much attention. These smaller, and often more typical efforts are illustrated here alongside the more major ones.

Colour Plate 2. *A royal visit to Sheerness in the reign of King William III. This is the type of small cabinet picture, well finished and most attractive, that Sailmaker produced in the 1679-1690 period. His typical 'restrained' palette is well illustrated here. Catalogue No.6.* OMELL GALLERY

Chapter 1
ISAAC SAILMAKER
1633-1721

Isaac Sailmaker was a shadowy and rather unknown figure in British marine painting right up to the early 1970s. Reading old catalogues and books prior to this date, he is often referred to as 'the father of British sea painting' or 'our first native sea painter', but these statements were not enlarged upon because so little was known about him. He lived from 1633 to 1721, a very long life span for those days, and he must have been painting for most of his adult life. But nobody knew how to identify his pictures with any degree of accuracy.

In general, any old marine picture that was painted before about 1720, and looked a little bit primitive, and which could not be definitely assigned to Van de Velde or any other early painter, was called an 'Isaac Sailmaker'. Thus his name became a sort of 'dust-bin attribution' for this type of painting in the hands of most salerooms and dealers.

One reason for this was that he never signed his pictures, and to this day

Plate 1. *Cromwell holding a baton, with a view of the great naval battle between Monck and Van Tromp, 2 and 3 June 1653. This is the earliest known painting attributed to Isaac Sailmaker. Catalogue No.32.* CHRISTIE'S

not one signed picture by him has turned up.

In the period from 1660 (restoration of Charles II) to about 1714 (death of Queen Anne) there were four specialist marine artists working in England apart from the great Van de Velde studio. These were Isaac Sailmaker (1633-1721), Jacob Knyff (1638-1681), J.K.D. van Beecq (1638-1722), and Adrian van Diest (1655-1704). Fortunately Van Diest and Van Beecq usually signed their pictures, so that we have a very good idea of their style.

However, up to 1970 no signed example of either Sailmaker or Jacob Knyff had appeared. There was an increasing number of these pictures appearing on the market and in various collections and there was considerable uncertainty as to which was the hand of Sailmaker and which was that of Jacob Knyff. It had already become apparent that there *were* two different hands at work – one rather better and more sophisticated than the other.

This puzzle was to a large extent solved in 1971 and 1972. In 1971 a

EDDYSTONE LIGHT HOUSE
being 90 Foot high 1783

Plate 2. *Engraving of the Eddystone Lighthouse. Inscribed lower left: Sailmaker den. – H. Hulsbergh Sculp. This is the second Eddystone light, known as Rudyard's Tower, which was completed in 1709. Note the rather haphazard sprinkling of the ships on the water in front of Plymouth harbour which is shown in the background. Catalogue Engraving No.5.*

painting of Rudyard's original Eddystone lighthouse with shipping around it turned up and this could be positively identified owing to its complete similarity to the Sailmaker print of this subject (Plates 2 and 3). Since then several other works obviously related to a Sailmaker print (for example, Plate 4) have appeared, which have consolidated the recognition of Sailmaker's hand.

Practically at the same time in 1972 a signed painting by Jacob Knyff appeared on the art market, which at once gave the essential clue to the identity of the other, and rather better hand (Colour Plate 7). Jacob Knyff (1638-1681) is known to have been working in England between 1672 and his death in 1681 and he is undoubtedly the author of the better and more sophisticated group of early marine pictures which had, up till then, been included in the general Sailmaker classification. Credit goes to Mr. E.H.H.

Colour Plate 3. *Portrait of the first* Britannia, *98 guns, under sail, in two positions. The* Britannia *was built at Chatham in 1682. She was the flagship of Admiral Sir Edward Russell at the Battle of Barfleur in May 1692. There is an almost identical 'twin' of this picture at the National Maritime Museum. They are two of Sailmaker's best ship portraits and were probably done about 1692 or so (his 'best period', during King William's reign). Catalogue No.15.*

CHRISTIE'S

Archibald[1], who was working at the National Maritime Museum at the time, for sorting out this tangle. Even now only one other signed Jacob Knyff has appeared, but it is enough to validate the new attributions.

It is rather extraordinary that these early and very competent marine painters working in England prior to about 1710 have received so little attention. The main reason is of course that in 1673 the Van de Veldes moved from Holland to England and set up their studio at Greenwich which rapidly dominated the marine painting scene. They were very good, and very prolific, and also enjoyed the royal patronage of Charles II and they inevitably became the stars of the marine painting firmament – and have in fact remained so ever since. Their works have been the subject of endless detailed study by art historians and scholars[2].

Let us now turn to Isaac Sailmaker. As his work can now be identified with relative certainty, an appraisal of his style and painting characteristics can be attempted with much more confidence. Since 1970 many more of his paintings have appeared, and so there is a reasonable body of his work available for study (see Catalogue at the end of this chapter).

1. E.H.H. Archibald. *Dictionary of Sea Painters*. Antique Collectors' Club, 2nd Edition, 1989.
2. M.S. Robinson, O.B.E. *The paintings of the Willem Van de Veldes*. Published by the Trustees of the National Maritime Museum, 1990.

Colour Plate 4. *Two Stuart royal yachts. An earlier picture, probably about 1675. A small, attractive 'cabinet picture'. The yacht on the left is probably the* Cleveland, *built for Charles II. Catalogue No. 42.* PRIVATE COLLECTION

Biographical Details

Much of this biographical material was researched by my daughter, Mrs. Judith Aldrick, BA.M.Litt., while she was working at the National Maritime Museum, some years ago. Her main sources were Vertue's Notebooks[3], apprentice lists, and census records.

According to Vertue, Sailmaker was born in Scheveningen in 1633. The original family name was Zeilmaker. He emigrated to London when he was very young and lived in the house of George Geldorf, an artist from Antwerp who came to London in 1623 and had a large house in Drury Lane. Geldorf apparently did very little painting himself, but was an entrepreneur and general art dealer who kept open house for foreign artists coming to live in London. Van Dyck and Peter Lely were both at some time his 'lodgers'. He was patronised by Charles I who made him a curator of the royal collection.

Thus young Isaac Sailmaker missed the rigorous and long apprenticeship

3. G. Vertue. Notebooks, 6 vols, 1715-1754. Published by the Walpole Society, Oxford.

to an established marine artist which he would have had in Holland. However he must have grown up in an artistic atmosphere, rubbing shoulders with many of the great artists of the period. He acted as assistant and general dogsbody to Geldorf and gradually absorbed some artistic training in this way.

After the execution of Charles I in 1649, Geldorf must have kept in touch with Cromwell, as the next thing we hear is that young Isaac Sailmaker was commissioned by the Protector himself to paint a view of the 'fleet before Mardyk' (which was ceded to England, together with Dunkirk, in 1658). Unfortunately this picture is untraced. But his first recorded picture dates from even before this (about 1653 – see Plate 1). This records the fight between Monck and Van Tromp, with Cromwell himself looking on from the left of the picture! Sailmaker must have been about twenty-one years of age when he did this.

In addition Trinity House own two large early ship portraits by him which must have been done in his early Cromwellian period. These are portraits of the *Sovereign of the Seas* and of the *Royal Prince* (Catalogue Nos. 20A and 20 and Colour Plates 9 and 10). The first of these, the *Sovereign of the Seas,* must rank as one of the earliest formal ship portraits in this country.

His master and patron, George Geldorf, survived the Restoration in 1660 and in 1662 was sworn in as 'Picture mender and cleaner' to Charles II. He died in 1665, three years later.

We know little of what happened to Isaac Sailmaker after this, but in 1695 his name appears in the census as living in the parish of Whitefriars with his wife Elizabeth and a daughter, also Elizabeth. In 1715 he had sufficient reputation to register an apprentice – one T. Mellor – at £15 a year! This was when he was over eighty and was, as Vertue puts it, 'painting to his last' – and perhaps finding a new demand for his work after the death of Van de Velde the Younger in 1707. He died at the great age of eighty-eight on 28 June 1721 at his house near the riverside outside the Temple Gate, called the King's Bench Walk.

In addition to the biographical notes Vertue also has a few pithy words about his artistic career. He comments:

> This little man employed himself always in painting views, small and great, many sea-ports and ships about England… He was a constant labourer… tho' not very excellent. His contemporaries the Van de Veldes were too mighty for him… but he outlived them and painted to his last.

Plate 3. *Sailmaker's oil painting of the same subject as in Plate 2. It was the comparison of the print and this painting which finally gave the essential clue to the Sailmaker painting style. Catalogue No.45.*   NATIONAL MARITIME MUSEUM

Colour Plate 5. *Stern view of a large English first-rate, with other shipping, in a calm sea. This pleasing little picture was painted after 1707. Catalogue No.49.* PRIVATE COLLECTION

Colour Plate 6. *Another pleasant little seascape by Sailmaker, from the 1680s, his best period. Oil on canvas. Catalogue No.35.* PRIVATE COLLECTION

Colour Plate 7. *This is the signed painting by **Jacob Knyff** which came to light in 1972 and provided the first definite evidence of what the hand of Knyff looked like. It is at once evident that this painting is much more sophisticated in construction than the average Sailmaker and the ships are painted more accurately. Catalogue No.6.* NATIONAL MARITIME MUSEUM

Vertue's remarks sum up his artistic career in a nutshell and could act as a rather moving little epitaph for him.

Sailmaker's artistic output may be considered under two headings, his prints and his paintings.

The Engravings

Eleven large line engravings after drawings by Sailmaker have been found and are catalogued at the end of this chapter. Nine of them are signed by Sailmaker and are thus definitely attributable. His name appears with various spellings – Sylmaker, Saylmaker and Sailmaker being the main variants. His drawings were engraved by several well-known engravers such as Kip, Van der Vucht and Hulsbergh.

Most of them belong to the later period of his life; seven were done after 1707, when he was in his early seventies. These were all topographical

Signature and date (1673), lower foreground of Colour Plate 7.

25

views of various ports and features round the south of Britain, such as Sheerness, Dover, Gravesend, Plymouth, Eddystone lighthouse, etc. They all depict numerous ships of all sorts, sprinkled about with the typical lack of accurate perspective which is one of the hallmarks of his work. Nevertheless, they are in fact attractive and accurate pictures and must rank as some of the best of his work.

The two big ship portraits were done a little earlier, in the reign of William and Mary (according to the royal standard depicted in the engravings).

The Battle of Malaga is a large engraving also (after 1704, the date of the battle) and a very good one. There is a Sailmaker painting at the National Maritime Museum which is identical with this print.

The Battle of Barfleur (1692) is an earlier engraving and not quite as accurate as the later ones.

The last four engravings listed in the Catalogue were commissioned for a large volume of engravings of places of interest in Great Britain which was published by Mortier[4] in 1724 (see Catalogue).

On the whole these engravings are accurate and must have been in great demand at the time they were done.

The Paintings

In making this assessment of Sailmaker, fifty-two photographs of his work have been found and examined, and of these about thirty of the original paintings have been seen. His subjects, in the paintings examined, were as follows:

    6 views of Greenwich
    3 views of Sheerness
    4 views of Portchester castle
    13 ship portraits
    5 battle scenes
    22 scenes of ships and yachts at sea, usually a calm or slightly ruffled sea, and usually two or more ships, with several smaller ones.

The views of Greenwich are particularly interesting as the Greenwich complex of Webb's buildings, the Observatory, and then Wren's buildings were all under construction in Sailmaker's lifetime. The six views of Greenwich can therefore be dated fairly accurately from the state of the

4. D. Mortier. *Nouveau Theatre de la Grande Bretagne,* 1714. (The Victoria and Albert Museum have a copy of this.)

A SEA FIGHT *between* Her Majesties *Royal Fleet, Commanded by the Right Hon.*ble *S*r *Geor: Rooke Vice Admiral of England &c . and the French Commanded by the Count de Thelouse in the Mediterranean*

Plate 4. *Engraving of the Battle of Malaga, 1704. Inscribed Sylmaker delin. Rooke in the* Royal Katherine *is shown alongside the large French flagship, the* Foudroyant. *(Note also the part played by the French galleys in towing the French ships in and out of the action.) An exact copy of this print as an oil painting by Sailmaker is at the National Maritime Museum, Greenwich. Catalogue Engraving No.1.*

buildings shown in the background, and thus the style of his paintings as the years progressed can be assessed. We find that the views painted prior to 1672 (Nos. 1–3 in Catalogue) are noticeably less well painted than those after 1675 (Nos. 4, 5 and 48). These latter are delightful and some of his best work.

There are two other ways of dating Sailmaker paintings. First there are the flags on the ships. In many of his ship portraits and some of his smaller paintings the royal standard is shown flying at the main mast-head. The standard of William III is easily recognisable – and the presence of this in a painting dates it to between 1689 and 1702. His later paintings are identified by looking at the red ensign which is usually flown on the stern of the ship. The earlier paintings show a plain red St. George's cross on a white ground in the 'fly' (that is, upper and inner corner) of the ensign. In 1707 this St. George's cross was modified by the addition of the white

Colour Plate 8. *An early Sailmaker battle scene. It probably represents the battle of Lowestoft (1665) – showing the moment after the Dutch flagship* Eendracht *blew up during its engagement with the Duke of York's flagship* The Royal Charles. The Royal Charles *is shown left foreground, with a boat picking up survivors of the sunken* Eendracht *from the water. Catalogue No.38.*   CHRISTIE'S

oblique St. Andrew's cross on a blue ground. This separates off a group of his paintings which were done *after* 1707 until his death in 1721 (Nos. 45–51 in the Catalogue).

The other, but rather less reliable, way of dating is where there is a ship portrait of a known named ship. The details of the launch, career, and fate of nearly every ship in the large Stuart navy are known, and can be found in Frank Fox's excellent book *Great Ships.*[5]

Using these methods of dating his pictures it immediately becomes apparent that the earlier pictures (before about 1675 or so) are much less

5. Frank Fox. *Great Ships.* The battle fleet of King Charles II. Conway Maritime Press Ltd., 1980.

Colour Plate 9. *The* Sovereign of the Seas. *This early ship portrait by Isaac Sailmaker shows her as she was before her major refit in 1651 (which altered her appearance particularly by the removal of the long beak at the bow). This means that Sailmaker could not have been much older than eighteen when he did this, and it must rank as one of the earliest English ship portraits. It is owned by and is on view at Trinity House in London. The* Sovereign of the Seas, *designed and built by Phineas and Peter Pett at Woolwich, was launched in 1637. She was the biggest and most expensive ship ever built at this time. The cost was so great that it led to the imposition of the unpopular tax known as 'ship money', which in turn was the spark which started the Civil War, which eventually lost Charles I his head. She served throughout the 2nd and 3rd Dutch Wars, and right into the 1690s at the Battles of Beachy Head and Barfleur. Then, in 1696, she was accidentally destroyed by fire. Catalogue No.20A.* TRINITY HOUSE, LONDON

well painted and structured than the later ones. It would appear that his draughtsmanship and general painting ability became better after about 1675, and the period covered by the reign of William III (1689-1702) seems to have been both his best and most prolific period. His best formal ship portraits such as the *Britannia* portraits (Catalogue Nos.14 and 15 and Colour Plate 3) and numerous charming little 'cabinet' pictures of Greenwich, Sheerness and royal yachts etc. belong to these years.

The sheer volume of his work is also quite impressive. There must be many more works in this country over and above the sixty-three prints and paintings which have been listed here.

Plate 5. *A fleet proceeding up channel with Dover and Dover Castle in the background. A large picture, well painted but showing the typical lack of perspective structure which is so typical of many Sailmaker pictures. Catalogue No.50* NATIONAL MARITIME MUSEUM

Characteristics of his Paintings

His earlier paintings (Catalogue Nos. 10, 11, 12, 20, 22 and 32) particularly show a certain primitive or almost amateur quality, both in the drawing and composition. He never, even later in his life, quite mastered the art of the use of perspective in structuring his pictures, and this must be the most basic characteristic to look for in identifying his works. When painting a number of ships sailing at sea (for example, Catalogue Nos. 45 and 50, Plates 3 and 5) the individual ships are painted accurately enough, but they seem to be scattered haphazardly over the canvas – sometimes with an obvious attempt at perspective which does not quite come off! For this reason some of his smaller pictures, which do not rely on perspective so much for their structure, appear much more attractive to the eye.

The other Dutch artists of the period, and particularly Jacob Knyff (with whom he is most likely to be confused up to 1681 when he died), used perspective much more successfully. The Van de Veldes, having been brought up in the painstaking Dutch school with long apprentice periods to a master such as Simon de Vlieger, were very successful in using perspective, which made their paintings more realistic and pleasing to the eye. This is of course where Isaac Sailmaker missed out; he never had the long rigorous apprenticeship period to an established Dutch Master.

Plate 6. *A royal yacht and a small merchantman off Greenwich. Webb's building, the completed observatory, and the spire of Greenwich parish church (which fell down in 1681) are all clearly seen. This therefore must have been painted between 1675 and 1681. Catalogue No.4.*

RAPHAEL VALLS GALLERY

Palette and Technique

The other main identifiable characteristic of his paintings is his palette and technique. Not for him were the colourful blue skies, pink clouds and wavy green seas of Jacob Knyff, J.K.D. van Beecq and Adrian van Diest. His palette was very restrained with grey clouds, and low key greens, and browns, and black and gold (for the decorated stern of ships) pre-dominating. In some of his smaller pictures he uses an intense luminous blue in the sky, which is very effective.

By far the most distinctive characteristic of his painting technique, however, is his method of applying the gold paint to the decorated sterns of his ships. The paint is applied in large dots or in what can only be described as 'long blobs', with a marked impasto – so that the gold blobs stand up and away from the paint surface. This gives his painting of the stern decoration a very characteristic 'dotted' appearance, and viewed obliquely you can see hundreds of small impasto blobs. All other artists of the period use normal flat brush strokes. This painting technique is the *most reliable single characteristic* by which his paintings may be identified.

Colour Plate 10. The Royal Prince. *The* Royal Prince *was launched at Woolwich in 1610, designed by Phineas Pett. During her long career she was rebuilt and modified several times. This portrait shows her as she was in about 1663. This must have been about the time when Sailmaker painted this portrait, which is also at Trinity House, London. She was named the* Resolution *during the Protectorate, but reverted to the name* Royal Prince *at the Restoration. She fought throughout the 2nd and 3rd Dutch Wars, but she ran aground and was captured and burned by the Dutch during the Four Days Battle in 1666. In this portrait she is wearing the Admiralty flag on the fore mast, the Stuart royal standard on the main mast, the Union on the mizzen mast and the red ensign at the stern. Catalogue No.20.* TRINITY HOUSE, LONDON

Flags

Another characteristic is in his painting of flags, which are nearly always spread out flat or stiff in the wind – this also contributes to the 'primitive' feel of his pictures. Most of the other artists of the period try and show flags and pennons curling in the wind. Occasionally a very restrained fold appears in some of his later flags, and a mild flutter in some of his pennons – but quite unlike the luxurious bends and curves which other artists give especially to the long flowing pennons from the mast-head.

One gets the impression, on surveying his work, that he started getting commissions from Cromwell and his associates at quite an early age – and there are four of his paintings (Catalogue Nos. 20, 20A, 22 and 32) which must have been done at this time when he was in his early twenties. Then, when Charles II came back, he fell out of favour – partly because of his association with Cromwell and partly because, as Vertue puts it, 'he was not very excellent' – particularly in comparison with the Van de Veldes and the other Dutch artists who flooded into England from 1672 onwards at the express invitation of Charles II.

His fortunes appear to have picked up when William and Mary came to the throne, and one suspects that he enjoyed quite a revival selling his pictures to the growing middles classes and lesser magnates who could not afford Van de Veldes. Certainly there was a big market for seascapes and ship pictures at this time when the Dutch, the French and the English all had huge navies which were pretty continuously in action one way or another. Also the East India Company was expanding, and interest in all forms of maritime activity was at an all time high. After the Van de Velde studio went into decline at the death of Van de Velde the Younger in 1707, Sailmaker was still actively painting and at last must have enjoyed a brief twilight of success in the absence of his great rival.

In 1990 a large and impressive ship portrait of the *Britannia* (Catalogue No.15, Colour Plate 3) by Sailmaker was sold at Christie's for £38,000. I can't help feeling that this 'Little man… a constant labourer… tho' not very excellent' would have derived some modest satisfaction from this belated tribute to his work!

Most Sailmaker paintings are in private collections, but the National Maritime Museum at Greenwich holds a very representative collection of twelve paintings by him.[6]

6. *Concise Catalogue of Oil paintings in the National Maritime Museum.* Antique Collectors' Club, 1988.

CATALOGUE OF PRINTS AND PAINTINGS
by
ISAAC SAILMAKER

Catalogue of Line Engravings from Drawings by Sailmaker

1. The Battle of Malaga, 1704. Signed 'Sylmaker Delin'. Published by J. Smith and R. Hulton. (There is an oil painting by Sailmaker identical with this print at the National Maritime Museum – Catalogue No.4.) *See Plate 4*

2. The Battle of Barfleur, 1692. This bears a cartouche in the sky which says 'A true draft of the great victory at sea gained by the English and Dutch over the French, May 19, 1692. Designed by I. Sailmaker according to the special direction of several on board during the action.'

3. The *Victory,* 100 guns (ex *Royal James*), as rebuilt in 1695. Engraving by Kip after I. Sailmaker.

4. The *Royal Prince* (later re-named *Royal William*). Inscribed 'I. Saylmaker delineavit'. Engraved by Van de Vucht.

5. Eddystone Lighthouse (Rudyards Tower, 1709). Inscribed 'Isaac Sailmaker den.' (There is an oil painting by Sailmaker identical with this print at the National Maritime Museum – Catalogue No. 45 and Plate 3.) *See Plate 2*

6. Sheerness. View with two large men-of-war and numerous smaller craft. Inscribed I. Saylmaker.

7. Gravesend. View from the sea with numerous small ships and one two-decker man-of-war. Inscribed 'Saylmaker del.' 'Kip Sculp.'

8. Plymouth. View from the sea, with numerous large men-of-war. Signed.

9. Dover and Dover Castle, the castle in the foreground. Signed 'Saylmaker del.'

10. A view of Chatham, numerous ships.

11. A view of Harwich and a bird's-eye view with numerous ships.

Note: Nos. 8, 9, 10 and 11 were done for Mortier's *Nouveaux Theatre de la Grande Bretagne* published in 1714.

Catalogue of Paintings

Views of Greenwich

1. View of Greenwich, showing Webb's building but no observatory. Two yachts, a small man-of-war, and a flute on the river. 13½in. x 26¼in. Christie's 24.7.80, Lot 100. Painted before 1672. Witt Library.

2. View of Greenwich, showing Webb's building but no observatory. A yacht and a large man-of-war, seen stern on, are in the forefront. This is a large and well painted and composed picture. 29½in. x 41¼in. Christie's 17.11.67, Lot 113. Painted before 1672. Witt Library.

3. View of Greenwich, showing Webb's building but no observatory. Two large men-of-war and two yachts in forefront. This is also a good picture. 33in. x 24in. Sold by Parker Gallery. Painted before 1672.

4. View of Greenwich, showing Webb's building *and* the observatory, and the spire of Greenwich parish church (which fell down in 1681). A royal yacht, and a small three-masted merchantman in foreground. A very well painted picture. 19¾in. x 29½in. Sotheby's New York 11.4.91, Lot 56. This must have been painted between 1675 and 1681.   *See Plate 6*

5. Large view of Greenwich, showing Webb's building to the *right* of the picture, and the observatory. A large yacht, stern on, heeling to the breeze in the centre, and a small three masted vessel to the right. Well painted. Size unknown. Location unknown. Photograph with author. Painted after 1675. (Also see Catalogue No.48.)

Views of Sheerness

6. A view of Sheerness, showing two royal yachts and a larger vessel stern on. One of the yachts flies the standard of King William III. Very attractive, well painted picture. 13½in. x 27½in. Panel. Christie's, July 1985. Later in Omell Gallery. Painted about 1690.
See Colour Plate 2

7. Shipping off Sheerness, in a rough sea. Three large warships and yacht, large rowing barge in foreground. Size unknown. Private Collection. Ref. *Country Life,* 12 May 1966.

8. Sheerness, showing a visit to the ships by King William III, in a yacht. Rough sea, but well painted. 42in. x 68in. At Ferens Art Gallery, Hull.

Views of Portchester Castle

9. Portchester Castle. Yachts (one with King William's standard) and a large vessel stern on, offshore. Good painting. 42½in. x 68in. With Leggatt, London. Ref. *Connoisseur,* November 1956. Painted after 1690.

10. Portchester Castle. Yachts and small man-of-war off shore, ruffled sea. Size unknown. Parker Gallery. Slightly more 'primitive'. Painted earlier?

11. Numerous (five) ships at sea, and a yacht, off Portchester Castle. Size unknown. N.M.M. photographic files (413621). Looks a little primitive and earlier.

12. Numerous (six) ships off Portchester Castle. rowing boat full of people in foreground. Size unknown (but large). N.M.M. photographic files (178-18). Also at Jacobs Gallery. Rather primitive, no perspective, probably an early painting.

13. Shipping off Portchester Castle. A long, narrow, quite small picture. Well painted. Private Collection.

Ship Portraits

14. The *Britannia* – stern and broadside view. 44in. x 57in. N.M.M. Collection. Painted about 1692.

15. The *Britannia*. Stern and broadside view. 30in. x 46¾in. Christie's 20.4.90, Lot 83. Now in a private collection, New York. This and the previous picture (No.14) are the two finest ship portraits done by Sailmaker. Painted about 1692.   *See Colour Plate 3*

16. Large fine portrait (in two positions) of a two-decker, with large rowing boats all around, possibly off Dover. Size unknown. Given by Yarrow & Co. to Glasgow University.

17. The *Lion*. Large portrait. 20in. x 33in. In possession of Rutland Gallery.

18. The *Royal Charles*. Broadside view only. Size unknown. In possession of Bristol City Art Gallery. (Also ref. Frank Fox's book *Great Ships* p.125.)

19. A large unframed three-decker, in two positions, at sea (no land). Size unknown. Good painting. Royal Collection.

20. The *Royal Prince*. An earlier, less fine portrait in two positions. Large. 66in. x 44in. Poor condition. (Note crew in tricorn hats). Owned by Trinity House. *See Colour Plate 10*

20A. The *Sovereign of the Seas*. A large (66½in. x 44in.) and very fine early portrait on panel. This ship was launched at Woolwich in 1637. The picture was originally a panel in the Mansion House (built in 1612, then rebuilt in 1678 at Blackwall Yard). It was presented to the corporation by C.H. Wigram Esq. in 1889. The crew are all shown wearing little red pointed woolly hats, as in the very early pictures. Owned by Trinity House. *See Colour Plate 9*

21. The *Royal Prince* and the *St. Michael* at the Battle of Texel (13 August 1673). The *Royal Prince* is shown badly damaged and dismasted. 33¼in. x 63½in. Sotheby's. 6.4.93, Lot 5.

22. The *Fairfax* and The *Tiger* – A large and less finished portrait. 39½in. x 37in. At N.M.M. An early work.

23. An East Indiaman. Striped flags (of East India Company). A large portrait. Two positions. N.M.M. Collection (BHC 1676). N.M.M. photographic files.

24. Large painting of five East Indiamen (striped flags). Size unknown. Christie's 21 March, 1975, Lot 104.

25. Another large portrait showing five East Indiamen (striped flags). Cartouche in sky says '1698 East India Ships 1683' and names of ships in left bottom corner.

Various Marine Scenes

26. A fleet, becalmed in the Downs. Size unknown. Parker Gallery. N.M.M. photographic files.

27. East India Company ships at anchor near docks at Deptford. Large painting, 36in. x 73in. – good picture. N.M.M. Collection (BHC 1873).

28. Ships in the Downs, some at anchor, others sailing. 20in. 32½in. Christie's 3.8.78, Lot 108.

29. English and Dutch ships at anchor in an estuary near a round fort (possibly Upnor Castle). Size unknown. N.M.M. photographic files.

30. Large painting of ships in line off a coastal town. Size unknown. N.M.M. photographic files.

31. A view of Chatham, panoramic. 28⅞in. x 35½in. Christie's 2.5.86, Lot 91.

32. A view of the great naval battle of 2-3 June between Monck and Van Tromp, with Oliver Cromwell, holding a baton, on the left of the picture. Now at the N.M.M. (BHC 2509). 15½in. x 20½in. Panel. Christie's 14.12.27 (Howarth Sale). *See Plate 1*

33. Landing of King William III at Torbay, November 1688. 37in. x 71in. N.M.M. (BHC 0326).

34. Small merchant ships off Dover. 23in. x 35in. Sotheby's 17.7.74, Lot 17.

35. English men-of-war and ketch-rigged yacht in a calm. 11¾in. x 25¾in. Christie's 30.1.87, Lot 85. Private Collection. *See Colour Plate 6*

36. Many English ships at sea off a low coast line. Christie's 10.12.71, Lot 129.

37. Landing of King William III at Torbay in 1688. 41in. x 70in. Sotheby's 16.11.83, Lot 18.

38. Battle between English and Dutch (possibly Battle of Lowestoft). 71½in. x 76¼in. Christie's 24.5.85, Lot 164. *See Colour Plate 8*

39. Large men-of-war, at anchor in a calm, seen from astern. 56in. x 53in. Painting at Saltram.

40. An English yacht (flying royal standard) passing another, at sea. Ship portrait type of painting. 34in. x 52in. N.M.M. Collection (BHC 0973).

41. A Stuart yacht and a merchant flute off a high headland. 18in. x 30in. Parker Gallery.

42. Two Stuart yachts, one stern on and one broadside, at sea. 11½in. x 15½in. Panel. Christie's 30.1.87. Private Collection. *See Colour Plate 4*

43. The *Fubbs* (ketch-rigged royal yacht) at sea, broadside on. 11½in. x 7½in. Panel. Private Collection.

44. Battle of Malaga. 15½in. x 20½in. Ex Caird Collection. Now at N.M.M. (BHC.0304).

After 1707

45. Eddystone Lighthouse, with Plymouth in the distance. Numerous ships. 49in. x 39in. N.M.M. photographic files. This is identical with the Sailmaker print (No.5 in this Catalogue and Plate 2). *See Plate 3*

46. Eddystone Lighthouse. Another smaller version of No. 45, with slight variations. N.M.M. photographic files.

47. Eddystone Lighthouse. Another much smaller version, with slight variations. On panel. Private Collection. N.M.M. photographic files.

48. A royal yacht off Greenwich. Must have been painted towards the end of his life, as it shows Wren's alterations almost completed.

49. Two three-deckers and a yacht at anchor in a calm. 11½in. x 13½in. Panel. Bonhams 12.8.92, Lot 540 C. Private Collection. *See Colour Plate 5*

50. Large three-decker, and another, with many accompanying ships proceeding up channel off Dover Castle. Attractive picture. 38½in. x 60in. Ex Caird Collection. Now in N.M.M. Collection (BHC 0972). *See Plate 5*

51. A large three-decker and other ships at sea, off Portsmouth, the steeple of St. Mary's church clearly visible. 33¾in. x 30½in. Sotheby's 6.6.84, Lot 153. Private Collection. Also illustrated in *Painters of the Sea* by David Cordingley.

52. Large topographical view of Chatham looking towards Rochester Castle. N.M.M. photographic files.

Plate 7. *An English ship, an English yacht and various small fishing vessels off Castle Cornet, Guernsey, Channel Islands. Catalogue No. 9.*   APPLEBY

Chapter 2
JACOB KNYFF
1638–1681

Jacob Knyff was the elder son of a good sea and river painter called Wouter Knyff, who was a pupil and imitator of Jan Van Goyen. Although usually classified as a minor master, Wouter Knyff was in fact very competent and prolific, and was an official of the Guild of Haarlem in 1675. His paintings were heavily influenced by Van Goyen and were good enough for many of them to be later attributed to the master himself. He had a long life (1607–1693) and a large family, of whom three became well-known painters in their own right. These three were Jacob Knyff (1638–1681), Willem Knyff (1646–1684) and Leonard Knyff (1650–1721).

The family was therefore an example of the dynastic painters of seventeenth century Holland, where the family talent was transmitted to the sons, who then received their early training in the family studio. The Knyff family is recorded as living first at Wesel, then in Haarlem (where Jacob was born), then at Middelberg and finally at Bergen-op-Zoom.

Willem appears to have stayed in Holland. Leonard (the youngest brother) emigrated to England quite early, probably in the 1670s, and settled in England (the public record office at Kew holds a record of his application for naturalisation papers in 1709). He of course became well

Plate 8. *A Dutch merchantman and other shipping (including an English man-of-war, an English yacht and fishing vessels) off Fort Elizabeth, Jersey, Channel Islands. This and the previous picture (Plate 7) were probably excuted in Knyff's middle period (about 1671) just before he emigrated to England. Catalogue No. 10.* APPLEBY

known in England for his paintings and meticulous plans and prints of many of the country houses and estates of the English aristocracy of the period.

Very little is known about Jacob's early life until 1670 when it is recorded that he had a studio in Paris. Soon after this, in 1672 or 1673, he came to England and stayed until his death in 1681.

By the time he arrived in Paris he was already a very competent and pleasing artist. There are two excellent paintings in the possession of the Trustees of Berkely Castle which must surely belong to those days, both signed and dated 1673. One is a lively scene of the river Seine in Paris, and the other a picture of Fontainbleau (see Catalogue Nos. 28 and 29).

What he was doing before he arrived in Paris is largely a matter of conjecture, but it is certain that for a large part of that time he must have been travelling round the Mediterranean. All his known earlier works are large, attractive, well painted Mediterranean harbour scenes (Catalogue Nos. 1-6 and Colour Plates 7, 11, 12 and 19).

The architecture of the ports is painted well and in great detail, as also are the ships. The harbours are full of Dutch traders, Spanish galleons, galleys, and an occasional British ship. The accuracy and competence with which he portrays the ships betray a long and sound sea-going experience. At the same time the general construction of these harbour scenes harks back to the training he must have had when helping his father in his studio in Haarlem to produce the river scenes with boats, towns and castles on the river bank, which were Wouter Knyff's stock in trade.

After 1673 his output appears to have been mostly British coastal or river scenes, with increasing emphasis on accurate and colourful depiction of the great ships of the Stuart navy. Later he even allows himself to paint pure ship portraits (Catalogue Nos. 19-22 and Colour Plate 16) with no land visible. He died in England at the relatively early age of forty-three, but no record has yet been found of the circumstances or cause of his early demise.

The Paintings

The following assessment of Jacob's work is based on a survey of thirty-five paintings which can be fairly definitely assigned to him (see Catalogue). There are at least four other works which are 'possibles', but they have been excluded from this assessment (although they are mentioned at the end of the Catalogue).

The subject matter of the pictures is as follows:

5 large Mediterranean harbour scenes
1 harbour scene off Calais
1 Mediterranean battle scene (English ships against Algerine pirates)
3 harbour scenes in the Channel Islands (showing Cornet Castle in Guernsey and Fort Elizabeth in Jersey)
7 showing English ships off Dover and Sheerness
7 showing English naval ships at sea with no (or very little) land visible

Colour Plate 11. *Dutch shipping in the roadstead of a Mediterranean port. Signed J.W.K. on stern of barge (left foreground). This is the typical composition of Knyff's earlier pictures, with 'pink' cloud masses much in evidence. Catalogue No. 1.*   PRIVATE COLLECTION

A view of the river at Chiswick
5 landscapes (various – see Catalogue)

Amongst these pictures there are six which bear a signature. Four of these are landscapes (Catalogue Nos. 28, 29, 30 and 32). These are signed either in full, or very shortly as J. Knyff (Catalogue No.32). Two of them are also dated 1673.

Only two of the seascapes are signed. One (Catalogue No. 6, Colour Plate 7) is fully signed – Jacob Knyff – and dated 1673. The other (Catalogue No. 1, Colour Plate 11) is an early Mediterranean harbour scene, and is initialled J.W.K. (Jacob Wouter Knyff). It is intriguing to wonder why he never signed any of his pictures after 1673. This embraced the whole of his 'English period', up to 1681. During this time he was most active producing many very large, colourful and rather prestigious pictures, which one might have thought would merit a signature. This lack of signature has had the inevitable result for posterity that it is difficult to identify his pictures until a fairly intensive study of his painting techniques and characteristics has been made. As we have seen in the previous chapter, for a long time his paintings were inextricably mixed up with those of Isaac

Colour Plate 12. *Another attractive early picture of a Mediterranean seaport scene. A Dutch trading vessel, a Spanish galleon and a galley are depicted very accurately in the foreground. Catalogue No. 2.*
PRIVATE COLLECTION

Sailmaker who was another non-signer. It is only within the last twenty years or so that this problem has been sorted out.

Characteristics of his Paintings

So we must now survey his pictures looking for the distinctive hallmarks which allow us to differentiate them from those of other marine artists of the period. We can look at these characteristics under five headings.

Size
He liked big pictures. Many of his canvases are very large indeed: 3ft.-4ft. x 5ft.-6ft. is quite common. Over three-quarters of the works surveyed come into this 'very large' category. It is really only towards the end of his English period that we find him producing smaller cabinet pictures, ship portraits of wonderfully high quality (Catalogue Nos.19-22 and Colour Plate 16).

Palette
His palette is very light and colourful. His skies are blue with very typical pink clouds. His seas usually have a greenish hue, and this, together with the gilded sterns of the great ships, and the numerous points of red on the inside of the open gun-ports, gives a very bright and colourful picture indeed. This is in sharp contrast to the rather restrained palette of Isaac Sailmaker, and even to most Van de Veldes. The Van de Velde sea often has

Colour Plate 13. *A large British two-decker, several yachts and smaller vessels, off Sheerness. This beautiful bright painting is typical of Jacob Knyff in his later English period (post 1672). The 'light' palette, the pink clouds, green sea, careful painting of the buildings on shore, and the depiction of the main ship from almost directly astern are all very typical features of these later paintings. Catalogue No. 11.* SOTHEBY'S

a bluish or even brownish tone to it, quite unlike that of Knyff. Only one other painter of the period approaches him in the 'brightness' of his pictures, and this is J.K.D. van Beecq. (Fortunately van Beecq usually signs, and has one or two other characteristics to know him by.)

His Drawing of the Ships
In all except five of his pictures the main big ship which is the focus of the composition is shown almost directly from the stern, with only very little of the port or starboard side showing, with numerous rather heavy and accentuated guns poking out of open gun ports (see Plate 8 and Colour Plates 13-15). The profile of these sterns is also highly typical with the side galleries accentuated and 'sticking out' to give a 'fat' appearance to the outline. In only four of his later paintings is the main ship depicted 'broadside on'.

His Drawing of the Sea
Most of his seas are calm and have a greenish texture with numerous little parallel ripples of white. But, in the few pictures of ships at sea, he is well able to portray realistic waves and the ocean swell. There are only two

pictures which have been tentatively assigned to him (Catalogue Nos. 33 and 34) which have very rough seas threatening to overwhelm or sink the ship (a set-up much beloved by most seventeenth century Dutch marine painters!).

Flags

His flags and pennons are well and realistically painted – usually fluttering in a light breeze. The 'flutter' of the mast-head pennons particularly is not overdone (as they usually are in the pictures of H. Vale). The St. George's cross in the fly of the red ensign on the stern is almost always painted in correct proportion to the rest of the flag (in sharp contrast to J. van Beecq who almost always paints it too small).

Altogether we have here a most competent and attractive artist. He was always most at home depicting his ships against the background of a port, or a castle, or some small town. He takes the same care in the painting of the architecture and busy figures of his ports as he does with the accurate portrayal of his great ships. He was essentially an 'all rounder' (to borrow a cricketing term), not just a specialist marine artist. In particular he was the

Colour Plate 14. *An English two-decker and a Dutch flagship off Dover. This again is a very large, light, attractive picture. Dover Castle and the town of Dover are shown in great detail. Catalogue No. 13.* PRIVATE COLLECTION

Colour Plate 15. *A large two-decker, flying the royal standard of Charles II, accompanied by three royal yachts, arriving at Dover (an extensive and detailed view of Dover town and castle). This picture probably commemorates the arrival at Dover of Mary of Modena for her marriage to James, Duke of York, in 1673. It is one of the biggest, most important and detailed pictures produced by Knyff in his English period. Catalogue No.16.* CHRISTIE'S

master of the big decorative recording of a special scene or event.

When all these characteristics are taken into consideration, he is fairly easy to recognise. Perhaps the most striking thing is the brightness and lightness of his pictures. It is almost as if he had transferred the whole scene to the Mediterranean summer, far away from our dull northern skies. A greater contrast to the grey tones of the great Dutch realist painters of the seventeenth century could hardly be imagined.

As a historical record painter he ranks very high indeed. The towns, castles and villages bordering his rivers and estuaries are well painted and accurate, showing just what they were like in those days. The same remarks go for his ships, which are nearly all careful portraits of real ships.

It is likely that he painted many more pictures than those listed here, but unfortunately he died young, aged forty-three, and this must inevitably have curtailed the number of his works. Also, his love of very large 'labour-intensive' canvases (and therefore time-intensive too!) must have been a factor in the relative rarity of his works.

Colour Plate 16. *The royal yacht* Sandadoes *at sea, flying the royal standard of King Charles II. One of his later, small cabinet pictures. Attractive, and of very high quality indeed. Catalogue No. 20.*
B. KOETSER

Colour Plate 17. *The Thames at Chiswick. A painting of great detail and historical reality, rather reminiscent of the riverscapes of his Dutch father, Wouter Knyff. Catalogue No. 7.*
BRIDGEMAN ART LIBRARY AND MUSEUM OF LONDON

Colour Plate 18. *An early work. Dutch East Indiamen off a southern coastline. A colourful, detailed and attractive picture. Catalogue No. 37. (In Musée des Beaux-Arts, Valenciennes, France.)*   BRIDGEMAN ART LIBRARY

Colour Plate 19. *Turkish and Dutch ships and galleys off an eastern port (Constantinople?). A typical scene and composition, a large picture. Catalogue No. 4.*   CHRISTIE'S

CATALOGUE OF PRINTS AND PAINTINGS
by
JACOB KNYFF

A necessarily rather rough attempt has been made to arrange the Catalogue in a probable chronological order. Thus his early Mediterranean harbour scenes come first followed by his 'English period'. His landscapes, however, are grouped together at the end (in spite of them having nearly all been done around 1673 – his mid-career).

1. Mediterranean harbour scene, with Dutch ships and galleys. Panel. 25¾in. x 47in. Signed J.W.K. on stern of one of the galiots. Sotheby's 26.10.88. The typical pink clouds and blue sky are much in evidence in this picture. Private Collection.   *See Colour Plate 11*

2. Dutch and Spanish ships and a galley off a Mediterranean port. Canvas. 26½in. x 48in. Bonhams 5.4.90, Lot 179. A very good picture typical of his early work. Private Collection.
See Colour Plate 12

3. Battle between English warships and Algerine pirates, off a rocky coast. Canvas. 28in. x 41in. Christie's 29.10.93, Lot 10. Private Collection.

4. Dutch and Turkish ships and galleys off an eastern port (Constantinople?). Canvas. 36in. x 76¾in. Christie's 23.4.82, Lot 29. (Illustrated in colour in *Dictionary of Sea Painters*, E.H.H. Archibald.[1]) Private Collection   *See Colour Plate 19*

5. Large English first-rate (possibly *Royal Charles)* with ships and galleys off a southern port (possibly Lisbon, depicting the departure of Katherine of Braganza in 1662). Canvas. A huge picture, 112in. x 191in. At N.M.M. (BHC 0935, illustrated in *Concise Catalogue*[2]).

6. English and Dutch ships taking on stores at a port. Canvas. 37in. x 49in. Signed in full and dated 1673. Christie's July 1972 . Now at N.M.M.   *See Colour Plate 7*

7. Chiswick, from the River Thames. Canvas. 32in. x 63in. An extremely fine and detailed painting, with his typical pink clouds much in evidence. Trustees of the London Museum.   *See Colour Plate 17*

8. Shipping off Castle Cornet, Guernsey (Channel Islands). Canvas. Large picture. Now housed in Castle Cornet as part of the Maritime Museum there.

9. Shipping off Castle Cornet. Very similar to No.8 above, but with different arrangement of ships. Canvas. Large picture. Was in the possession of a Jersey dealer (Appleby's).
See Plate 7

10. Shipping off Fort Elizabeth, Jersey (Channel Islands). Christie's 8.2.63, Lot 102. Canvas. Large picture, 37in. x 40in. Was in the possession of a Jersey dealer (Appleby's).
See Plate 8

11. The fleet off Sheerness. Canvas. 42½in. x 69in. Sotheby's July 1986, Lot 11. A large, bright, attractive picture.   *See Colour Plate 13*

12. Another, not so good, version of No.11 above (fleet off Sheerness). Canvas. 50½in. x 71½in. In National Gallery of Ireland (No.1741).

13. A large picture of an English and a Dutch flagship, off Dover. Calm sea. Canvas. 35in. x 71in. Christie's 12.5.67, Lot 48. Formerly the property of Lady Belhaven.
See Colour Plate 14

1. E.H.H. Archibald. *Dictionary of Sea Painters*. Antique Collectors' Club, 2nd Edition, 1989.
2. *Concise Catalogue of Oil Paintings in the National Maritime Museum*. Antique Collectors' Club, 1988.

14. A slightly smaller picture, English warships in a 'slightly rough' sea off Dover. Canvas. 24in. x 48in. Ex Collection Major R.C. Sloane Stanley (also once in the possession of F. Sabin).

15. Large British second-rate warship, and other small ships, off Dover (extensive view of harbour and castle). Wavy sea. Canvas. 19½in. x 48in. Sotheby's 12.3.80, Lot 11.

16. A two-decker (flying Charles II royal standard) off Dover (extensive view), with royal yacht. Calm sea. Canvas. 47¼in. x 68in. Christie's 26.4.85, Lot 77. Formerly owned by Bishop of Armagh. This picture probably commemorates the arrival at Dover of Princess Mary of Modena for her marriage to James, Duke of York in 1673. An exceptionally fine and detailed picture. (Illustrated in Gavin, *Royal Yachts,* 1932.[3])   *See Colour Plate 15*

17. Charles II and James, Duke of York visiting the *Royal Sovereign,* in the royal yacht *Cleveland,* for a Council of War at the Nore, 1673. Canvas. 25in. x 30in. Formerly in the possession of the Parker Gallery. Also see Plate 10, p. 49, Frank Fox's *Great Ships.*[4]

18. An English two-decker, and escorting yachts, off Calais. Canvas. 43in. x 72in. Thought to be Mary of Modena, leaving Calais for England in 1673. N.M.M. (BHC 0319, illustrated in Concise Catalogue[2]).

19. The *Cleveland* royal yacht (flying the royal standard and seen broadside on) with other warships at sea. Calm sea. Canvas. Size unknown. Private Collection, Canada. N.M.M. photographic files.

20. The royal yacht *Sandadoes* (flying the royal standard of Charles II), at sea. Shown 'broadside on', with other shipping. Wavy sea. Canvas. 18in. x 30in. Formerly in the possession of B. Koetser and then F. Sabin.   *See Colour Plate 16*

21. Another very similar version of No. 20 above, but with different accompanying ships. Royal yacht *Sandadoes* at sea. Wavy sea. Canvas. 18in. x 30in. Sotheby's 14.3.90, Lot 1 (withdrawn).

22. A two-decker and a galiot at sea (broadside on), wavy sea. Canvas. 18in. x 30in. In the possession of B. Koetser and then F. Sabin.

23. There are at least four marine pictures in the Berkely Castle Collection which have until recently been attributed to William van de Velde the Elder. Two, however, have all the characteristics of J. Knyff paintings, especially his palette. Berkely Castle possesses three large landscapes (Catalogue Nos. 28, 29 and 30) signed by Jacob Knyff and dated 1673 and it is therefore quite likely that Jacob Knyff was working for the Berkelys at that time and could have done the ship paintings as well.

24. Large ship portrait of the *Royal Prince,* about 1680, with other shipping. Canvas. Size large. A good picture. Private Collection. N.M.M. photographic files.

25. The *Royal Sovereign* at sea. Canvas. Size unknown. Private Collection. Now Courtauld Institute.

25A. The *Royal Prince* and yacht *Henrietta,* off Dover. Fairly rough sea. 25in. x 28in. Was in the possession of F.T. Sabin (dealer).

26. Return of the *Mary Rose.* Canvas. 31in. x 21in. Bonhams 9.5.74, Lot 212.

27. A fleet at sea. Canvas. 16in. x 24in. Previously attributed to Antonio Verrio. Illustrated in *Old Sea Paintings* by Keble Chatterton, p.94.[5] Now at N.M.M.

3. C.M. Gavin R.N. *Royal Yachts,* Rich and Cowan Ltd., 1932. Limited Edition.
4. Frank Fox. *Great Ships.* The battle fleet of King Charles II. Conway Maritime Press Ltd., 1980.
5. E. Keble Chatterton. *Old Sea Paintings.* Clowes and Sons Ltd., 1928.

Landscapes

28. The Seine in Paris, showing the Louvre with numerous small ships. Canvas. Signed and dated 1673. Owned by the Berkely Castle Trustees.

29. 'Fontainbleau'. Canvas. Signed and dated 1673. Owned by the Berkely Castle Trustees.

30. Durdans House, Epsom. Attractive large picture. Canvas. 40in. x 72in. Owned by the Berkely Castle Trustees.

31. Landscape with windmill. Canvas. Size unknown. In Dublin. Witt Library.

32. A small view in Warsaw. Canvas. Signed (but not dated). Witt Library.

Possible Other Works

33. A British second-rate labouring in very heavy seas near a coastal fortress. Canvas. 40in. x 64in. Phillips 20.4.93, Lot 44.

34. British ships in very rough seas near a jetty. Canvas. 29½in. x 37½in. Sotheby's 18.11.92, Lot 164.

35. A view of Dordrecht, with an English yacht in foreground, and two Dutch merchantmen and numerous other small vessels. Canvas. 20in. x 43in. Sotheby's 4.7.84, Lot 13. Private Collection.

36. A large first-rate, off a coastline, loading stores from longboats on beach. Size large. Private Collection.

37. Two Dutch East Indiamen and a small Levanter, off a Mediterranean coastline, near an estuary. An early picture, well detailed, with a very blue sky, and very striking and attractive. Canvas. Size large. At Musée des Beaux-Arts, Valenciennes, France.

See Colour Plate 18

Colour Plate 20. *Portrait of the* Royal Prince. *Signed and dated 1679. His accuracy and the general lightness of his palette can be appreciated well here. This is undoubtedly one of his best ship portraits. Catalogue No. 8.*   NATIONAL MARITIME MUSEUM

Chapter 3
JAN KAREL DONATUS VAN BEECQ
1638-1722

Of the small group of specialist marine painters who were working in England between approximately 1670 and 1720 none was more thoroughly competent and technically finished than Jan Karel Donatus van Beecq. In view of this, it is perhaps rather astonishing that so little is known about his life and background.

He was born in Holland in 1638 and died there in 1722. Most of his working life, however, appears to have been divided between France and England. It is known that he came to England from France some time after 1672, probably in response to Charles II's invitation to Dutch artists to come to work in this country. Research on his work and artistic style is facilitated because no fewer than twelve of the twenty-five pictures by him which are available for study in this country are clearly signed and dated. The task of evaluating his work and general style is made much easier by this – and is in marked contrast to Isaac Sailmaker and Jacob Knyff, for instance, who practically never signed their pictures.

We also know that, after working in England for a few years, he returned to Paris in 1681 and worked for his French patron, the Duc de Vendôme at the Château de Marly, for a time. He was also elected a member of the French Academy at this time.

It seems likely, from studying the dates on his pictures, that he made several visits to England before his death in Holland in 1722. A large group of his English pictures are dated 1677, 1678 and 1679. Some French pictures in the Palais de Chaillot are dated 1684, which fits in with the fact that we know he was working in France at that time. However, there are three English pictures which are dated 1689 and 1701, suggesting that he

Plate 9. English men-of-war, in a calm sea. Signed and dated 1677. *Note the studied accuracy of the painting in all its detail, giving it an almost photographic appearance. Catalogue No. 2.*
MUSEUM OF FINE ART, COPENHAGEN

Plate 10. An English first-rate (with C.R. on stern) with two other ships and numerous rowing boats. Signed I.V.B. on right. Catalogue No. 14.

might have returned to England for a further period round about these dates. It is recorded that he finally left Paris in 1714.

So it would appear that he divided his time between England and France during the later years of his life. This would account for the fact that a large part of his work has found its way into collections all over Europe – France, Germany, Malta, Denmark – as well as England.

We are fortunate in having now a significant part of his work – amounting to twenty-five pictures – available for study from English records (such as the Witt Library, the National Maritime Museum and the records of salerooms such as Christie's, Sotheby's, Phillips and Bonhams).

The Paintings

The following evaluation of his style is based on the study of twenty-seven of his paintings. Many of these have appeared in English salerooms during the last thirty years or so. Some of them have been seen personally by the author, and good photographs of the others have been obtained and studied. The others are to be seen in various museums. The National

Detail of the I.V.B. signature in Plate 10.

Colour Plate 21. *A smack-rigged royal yacht, an English two-decker (seen stern on) and other units of the fleet in the distance. This is a most attractive and typical picture. The green sea, the red ensign with the St. George's cross in the fly which is shown too small, and the wavy mast-head pennons are all very typical Van Beecq characteristics. This painting is not signed and for a long time was thought to be by Isaac Sailmaker. Catalogue No. 23.* CHRISTIE'S

Maritime Museum has two good examples, as also has the Danish National Museum in Copenhagen and the French Maritime Museum at the Palais de Chaillot in Paris.

Van Beecq appears to have been a true specialist marine painter, because nineteen of these pictures are of ships at sea with little or no land visible. There are two rather crowded battle scenes and there are five of ships in an estuary or close to land, where a more or less sketchy area of land is indicated. This is in great contrast to the pictures of Jacob Knyff, and Sailmaker in particular, in which the ships are often depicted off a well-known port (such as Dover or Greenwich) and the features of the land are carefully and lovingly depicted.

Characteristics of his Paintings

Van Beecq was a highly individual craftsman and there is no evidence that he copied the Van de Veldes, or was even influenced by them. Most of his subjects are individual ship portraits in their natural setting (i.e. at sea).

His painting technique is very good, the paint being laid on flat and accurately. This can be studied and admired in his best ship portrait (Colour Plate 20), the *Royal Prince,* at the National Maritime, Museum, Greenwich, signed and dated 1679. This same picture gives a very good idea of his palette, which is light and colourful, giving the picture a very

Colour Plate 22. *An English royal yacht passing by a Dutch fishing fleet at sea. Signed and dated 1678. An exceedingly fine picture, demonstrating his ability to paint a choppy sea realistically. Catalogue No. 6.* MARTYN GREGORY

striking, attractive appearance.

Looking over the twenty-seven paintings as a whole, certain very recognisable characteristics stand out. Light blue skies with natural looking white or grey clouds are common. His seas have a greenish hue and are very realistic, ranging from calm with small ripples to a full blown ocean swell which is very well done. This competent and realistic rendering of the sea is a major feature of most of his pictures (see Plate 12 and Colour Plate 22).

His Drawing of the Ships
The drawing of the ships is excellent and accurate as he is a fine draughtsman. If there is a fault from the artistic point of view, it is that all detail is shown too accurately; also the ships have a rather low and elongated appearance. This tends to make the composition rather stilted (Plate 9), almost as if one was looking at a fine collection of models rather than real ships.

Plate 11. *Royal yachts at sea, with units of the fleet at anchor in the background. A beautiful, breezy picture, with a choppy sea in typical Van Beecq style. Not signed. Catalogue No. 21.*

Plate 12. *The junction of Admiral D'Estrées with the Duke of York's fleet just before the Battle of Sole Bay in 1672. This picture is signed and dated 1684, and is in the French National Maritime Museum, Palais de Chaillot, Paris. Catalogue No. 10.*

FRENCH NATIONAL MARITIME MUSEUM, PALAIS DE CHAILLOT, PARIS

Plate 13. *An English man-of-war, with several other Dutch vessels lying in a calm estuary, off a small Dutch port. Signed and dated 1677. This is the only one of all his pictures which shows the St. George's cross in the fly of the ensign on the mainmast depicted too big! Catalogue No. 3.*
CHRISTIE'S

Flags

In painting the flags he has one idiosyncrasy which can be reliably used in identifying his paintings. In painting the red ensign, which is usually on the stern of his ships, the St. George's cross in the 'fly' of the ensign is almost always shown too small (Plate 11 and Colour Plates 20-22). There is only one of the twenty-seven paintings in which this characteristic is not present (Catalogue No. 3 and Plate 13) and in this one (a signed one) the St. George's cross is suddenly shown much too big! The pennons from the mast-head are often drawn curling in the wind.

Figures

The drawing of his figures – either on board or in small attendant rowing boats – is usually very good and detailed, each one doing something appropriate.

Altogether we have here a very fine marine painter, with a sophisticated technique, producing a large number of accurate ship portraits in their natural setting. It is likely that he produced many more works than those

57

Colour Plate 23. *Two men-of-war, with other small craft riding at anchor off Greenwich. Note the rather sketchy depiction of Greenwich, which obviously takes very second place to the ship portraits. Catalogue No. 22.*

SOTHEBY'S

Colour Plate 24. *A large battle scene, thought to be the battle of La Hogue. Catalogue No. 25.*
PRIVATE COLLECTION

Colour Plate 25. *An unusually large picture of English and Dutch shipping beside a harbour and a town, unidentified. It is signed and dated 1677. Catalogue No. 27.* SOTHEBY'S

Plate 14. *Shipping in the Bristol Avon. Signed and dated 1701. This is the last signed and dated picture by Van Beecq. Note the quite unusual amount of detail given to a large quantity of land in the picture. Catalogue No. 13.* NATIONAL MARITIME MUSEUM

listed in the catalogue because his paintings are popular and widely scattered in private collections all over Europe and also in the U.S.A., but particularly in France. These are exceedingly difficult to trace.

Most of his paintings are of small to moderate size (so-called cabinet paintings) which probably reflects the type of client for whom he worked. This would have been the emerging middle class, merchants, shipping firms, sea captains, etc., rather than the 'nobility' who would have had large wall spaces to fill.

The only exception to this was a very large painting of English and Dutch ships off what looks like a Dutch port (see Colour Plate 25, Catalogue No. 27). This was sold at Sotheby's on 13 July 1994, Lot 5. It measured 32½in. x 72¼in. and was exceptionally large.

CATALOGUE OF PAINTINGS
by
JAN KAREL DONATUS VAN BEECQ

The sources from which this catalogue is constructed are detailed at the end of it. The first thirteen pictures are signed and dated and are therefore presented in chronological order.

1. A large English man-of-war at anchor on right, with several smaller ones sailing on left. Canvas. 31⅛in. x 12½in. Signed and dated 1677. Museum of Fine Arts, Copenhagen.

2. English men-of-war, quarter stern view, in a calm at sea. Large warship and rowing barge in forefront of picture. Canvas. 31⅛in. x 12½in. Signed and dated 1677. Museum of Fine Arts, Copenhagen. *See Plate 9*

3. An English man-of-war, with several other Dutch vessels, lying in a calm estuary, off a small Dutch (?) port. Canvas. 23½in. x 35½in. Signed and dated 1677. Ex-property of Dowager Lady Camoys. Christie's 11.12.81, Lot 20. *See Plate 13*

4. Large English two-decker, seen from stern quarter, in foreground, with rowing barge and two yachts. Fully rigged. Canvas. 33½in. x 39½in. Signed and dated 1677. In 1971 was in the possession of W.H. Paterson (a London dealer).

5. Dutch and English vessels becalmed in the Straits of Messina, off Sicily, with Mt. Etna in the background. Panel. Signed and dated 1677. Private Collection in Scotland.

6. An English royal yacht passing by a Dutch fishing fleet at sea. Canvas. 22in. x 34½in. Signed and dated 1678. Sotheby's, Ireland, Mount Juliet, 20.10.87, Lot 71. In the possession of London dealer Martyn Gregory. This is an exceptionally fine picture and very typical of Van Beecq. *See Colour Plate 22*

7. An English first-rate warship seen broadside on, with a barge in the foreground. Canvas. 35½in. x 21¼in. Signed and dated 1679. National Museum of Malta. This painting is in poor condition.

8. A portrait of the *Royal Prince* in a calm sea, with yachts and other vessels in the background. Canvas. 22in. x 35½in. Signed and dated 1679. N.M.M.. An exceptionally fine, bright, well-painted portrait. *See Colour Plate 20*

9. Admiral Duquesne's fleet mopping up the Algerian pirates at Tripoli in 1680. Canvas. Signed and dated 1684. French National Maritime Museum, Paris (Palais de Chaillot).

10. The junction of D'Estrées with the Duke of York's fleet, just before the Battle of Sole Bay in 1672. A large French flagship in left foreground. Canvas. Signed and dated 1684. French National Maritime Museum, Paris (Palais de Chaillot). *See Plate 12*

11. A British flagship, royal barge and other vessels. Canvas. Signed and dated 1689. Christie's 30.1.70.

12. British two-decker and yachts off Greenwich. Canvas. 61½in. x 54½in. Signed and dated 1689. Sotheby's 18.11.87, Lot 5. Was in the possession of Alan Jacobs Gallery, London.

13. Shipping in the Bristol Avon. Canvas. 36in. x 46in. Signed and dated 1701. N.M.M. *See Plate 14*

14. An English first-rate (with C.R. on stern) and two other ships in the background – numerous rowing boats, calm sea. Canvas. 12in. x 15in. Signed I.V.B. (not dated). Formerly Author's Collection. *See Plate 10*

Further pictures, which can stylistically be assigned to Van Beecq with confidence, but which are not signed.

15. Broadside view of a one-decker, French (?) man-of-war in an estuary, calm sea. Canvas. In National Maritime Museum, photographic files. A good picture, very typical.

16. A French two-decker with a galley, both seen broadside on. Canvas (large picture). N.M.M. photographic files. The picture is said to be in a Copenhagen collection.

17. An English second-rate, seen broadside on, at sea. Canvas. 25½in. x 18½in. N.M.M. photographic files. Private Collection, Germany.

18. A good starboard broadside portrait of an English two-decker (possibly an East India-man). Canvas. Christie's 14.2.72, Lot 192 (catalogued as Van de Velde).

19. Two large French men-of-war. Canvas. 31in. x 43in. Sotheby's 28.11.73, Lot 179. N.M.M. photographic files. Present location unknown.

20. Royal yachts in an estuary, larger ships in background, rowing barge in foreground. Canvas. Was in the possession of Sabin (dealer). This is the only picture found which shows the boats flying the *post 1707 red ensign*. One yacht is shown flying the Royal standard of Queen Anne.

21. Royal yachts at sea, wavy sea, fleet in background. Canvas. Phillips Son & Neale 25.11.68, Lot 96. A big, colourful picture, very typical of Van Beecq, but not signed.

See Plate 11

22. Two men-of-war and other small craft riding at anchor off Greenwich. Canvas, 61½in. x 54½in. Was owned by Miss Marion Davies and exhibited in Los Angeles County Museum. Sotheby's 18.11.87, Lot 5 (£14,500). *See Colour Plate 23*

23. A smack-rigged royal yacht and an English two-decker (stern on), other units of the fleet in the distance. Canvas. 29½in. x 58in. Christie's 20.4.90, Lot 81 (catalogued as Isaac Sailmaker). A very typical Van Beecq. *See Colour Plate 21*

24. Embarkation of Isabella at Lisbon to marry Charles II. An unusually large amount of harbour is shown here. Canvas. Witt Library.

25. Large battle scene (possibly La Hogue). Canvas. 29in. x 40in. Ex Rothschild Collection (previously catalogued as L.d. Man). Private Collection. *See Colour Plate 24*

26. Print of a large 'Battle of La Hogue'. Seen in France. Location of original unknown.

27. English and Dutch shipping beside a harbour with large handsome buildings. Canvas. 32½in. x 72¼in. Signed and dated 1677. Sotheby's 13.7.94, Lot 5. *See Colour Plate 25*

Sources from which the Catalogue was compiled

1. National Maritime Museum, Greenwich.
2. Fine Art Museum, Copenhagen.
3. French National Maritime Museum, at Palais de Chaillot, Paris.
4. Catalogues of Christie's, Sotheby's, Phillips and Bonhams over past twenty-five years.
5. Picture dealers' catalogues (particularly Alan Jacobs, Sabin, Martyn Gregory, W.H. Paterson, all of London.)
6. National Museum of Malta.
7. Personal collection.

Colour Plate 26. *This large painting belongs strictly to Van Diest's landscape group. It shows a loaded wherry being towed along a river by a horse on the river bank, with a castle and landscape beyond. Not signed.* CHRISTIE'S

Chapter 4
ADRIAN VAN DIEST
1655–1704

Adrian van Diest is a little different from the other artists considered in this series because he was very much a 'universal' painter. He turned his hand to landscapes, harbour and coastal scenes, seascapes, ship portraits, animals and ordinary portraits, with equal facility.

He painted very much for the market and so there are a great many paintings of small size and of shapes to fit a particular place in a room – such as his long, low 'over-door' pictures. But he was perfectly capable of painting pleasing pictures of large or small size.

He has often been categorised as 'mostly a landscape painter'. However,

Plate 15. *An English two-decker off the coast, with a large rock to the right, which is surmounted by a primitive 'lighthouse'. In the left lower corner are the two typical fisherman figures, casting a net, which appear in many of Adrian van Diest's pictures. Signed with initials A.V.D. Catalogue No. 17.*
CHRISTIE'S

Plate 16. *This large picture shows the action between the* Mary Rose *and her escorts and seven Algerine pirate vessels in December 1669. It is initialled A.V.D. on the back of the canvas and is a more or less straight copy of a picture by William van de Velde the Younger which is in the Royal Collection. Catalogue No. 18.*
THE LEGER GALLERIES LTD.

Colour Plate 27. *This large and attractive 'Southern Harbour Capriccio' is very typical of the more finished examples of his work. The large English two-decker firing a signal gun wears a pre-1707 red ensign. There are elegant figures of merchants in the foreground, also a typical Mediterranean galley, and other shipping. The landscape and hills fade into the distance on the right and on the left is his typical tree with 'feathery' leaves. Fully signed. Catalogue No. 4.* CHRISTIE'S

his scope is well illustrated by the excellent photographic collection in the Witt Library and my own photographic collection, comprising a total (from both sources) of eighty-seven pictures. The subjects are as follows:

62 pure landscapes (often with numerous figures, cows, a sheep, etc.)
17 harbour or coastal scenes (of Mediterranean type) with large well-painted English ships and galleys
10 sea battle scenes, or individual ships at sea

In addition to the above, the author has seen two portraits and a dog portrait.

Biographical Details
He was born at the Hague in 1655, the youngest son of an established

Colour Plate 28. *This smaller and similar southern harbour capriccio is a good example of his less important quickly produced pieces. The general formula is the same as Colour Plate 27 and the large figures in the foreground (two fishermen and two maidens) are well done. Unsigned. Catalogue No. 13.* PRIVATE COLLECTION

Dutch marine painter, William van Diest (1610-c.1663). His elder brother, Jeronymus van Diest (1631-1673) was also an accomplished marine painter who liked large canvases and whose style was a great influence on Adrian's marine paintings.

Adrian arrived in England in 1672 at the age of seventeen. He rapidly found patrons, including King Charles II who owned five of his works. The Earl of Bath employed him, and even Sir Peter Lely was found to possess seven of his works at his death in 1680.

This was an age when the concept of an 'Ideal Landscape' as a subject for an attractive painting was gaining favour, much influenced by the work of Claude Lorraine. Adrian van Diest seems to have taken up this idea enthusiastically as much of his work in England consists of attractive capriccio landscapes and harbour-scapes. He must have found a ready market for this

Colour Plate 29. *This delightful little seascape, showing an English two-decker on the right and a lugger reducing sail in the left foreground, is one of his best and most attractive marine pictures. Signed bottom right. Catalogue No. 15.* PHILLIPS

type of work as he produced a large quantity of them and, judging by the present-day market, the public finds them as attractive now as they did then.

It is recorded that he had many ups and downs during his life in England, and that some of his works were rushed out in a hurry in order to keep the wolf from the door. He died at the age of forty-nine, badly affected by gout, and was buried somewhere below St. Martin's church, with no known monument.

It is still possible to find an Adrian van Diest, lurking in a corner, or over a door or window, in many of the old houses in England, Scotland and Ireland – usually unrecognised or miscatalogued. The last one spotted by the author was over a window at 'The Vyne' in Hampshire – one of his typical little coastal scenes. It was a long and low picture, the shape being obviously suited to the situation where it was to hang.

Colour Plate 30. *This is one of his typical long narrow harbour capriccio scenes, designed for an 'over-door' or 'over-window' situation. The English ship is there, as usual, and the foreground is peppered by small figures fishing from the beach. To the right is a small walled town. Not signed. Christie's 1.3.91, Lot 111.* CHRISTIE'S

The Pictures

We are basically concerned here with his seascapes and harbour scenes rather than his landscapes. His harbour scenes are produced almost according to a formula, but in spite of this they are very colourful and attractive.

Colour Plates 27 and 28 show two typical examples. It is rather astonishing that nearly all these harbour scenes depict a Mediterranean harbour rather than an English one, and the figures and landscape are typically southern. In spite of this, there is always an English ship in the harbour, often surrounded by typical Mediterranean galleys. In the foreground are often many well-painted figures, or herdsmen with cattle. To the left there is almost always a tree overhanging the scene with very typical feathery leaves. Colour Plates 27 and 28 are two good examples. The latter is one of his quick small 'formula' paintings while the former is one of his more elaborate efforts with a good deal of detail.

Twelve out of seventeen are signed. He signs either A. Diest or A.V. Diest, or in monogram style AD or AVD with the three letters run together.

The next group of his pictures are those more specially 'marine' in flavour. There are six depicting battle scenes and four depicting a ship or ships at sea, with either no land or a small amount of land quite secondary to the depiction of the ship.

Of particular interest is his painting of the *Mary Rose* action. This is a straight copy of a well-known painting in the Royal Collection by W. van de Velde the Younger, but it is signed on the back of the canvas with the initials A.V.D. This gives some weight to the assumption made by certain authors (see Robinson[1] and Archibald[2]) that Adrian van Diest found some employment as a 'copyist' or studio assistant in the Van de Velde studio at Greenwich, although there is no documentary evidence for this. His *Battle of Bantry Bay* (Colour Plate 33) is also derived from a Van de Velde composition.

The remaining four paintings of ships at sea appear to be entirely his own work. Colour Plate 29 is a particularly charming and accurate little seascape, which shows how good he could be when he tried.

Fortunately the majority of his works are signed, but the occasional unsigned work showing ships alone may be quite difficult to differentiate from a Van de Velde. However, his figures (if present) will usually give the clue to the artist (Colour Plate 31).

Adrian van Diest was the acknowledged master of the 'capriccio' harbour or coastal scene, usually with a British ship as one of the central objects. He was exceedingly colourful and realistic in his rendering of these. It is a pity that he did not have many more commissions for ship portraits and 'pure' marine scenes, but there was so much good competition for these works from the great Van de Velde studio, and the other marine artists mentioned here, that he really never got much of a chance to develop this aspect of his art.

Nevertheless, he richly deserves his place as one of the major marine artists working in England in the last quarter of the seventeenth century.

1. M.S. Robinson, O.B.E. *The paintings of the Willem Van de Veldes*. Published by the Trustees of the National Maritime Museum, 1990.
2. E.H.H. Archibald. *Dictionary of Sea Painters*. Antique Collectors' Club, 2nd Edition, 1989.

Colour Plate 31. *An English two-decker warship, in two positions, at sea. This picture is not signed, but the little figures casting nets in the lower right-hand corner are so typical and appear in so many A. van Diest pictures that they almost constitute a signature in themselves. Catalogue No. 16.*
CHRISTIE'S

Colour Plate 32. *The destruction of the French ships at La Hogue, just after the Battle of Cape Barfleur in 1692. In this action twelve French ships were burned and destroyed and it effectively ended any hopes that the exiled James II had of regaining the throne. It is the best of Adrian van Diest's large set piece battle scenes. Catalogue No. 21.*
NATIONAL MARITIME MUSEUM

Colour Plate 33. *The Battle of Bantry Bay, 1689. The French fleet was found in Bantry Bay, delivering stores for the exiled King James's army in Ireland. The English under Admiral Herbert (later first Earl of Torrington) attacked them, resulting in an indecisive action, the first in the so-called War of English Succession 1689-1697. Catalogue No. 19.*
NATIONAL MARITIME MUSEUM

CATALOGUE OF PAINTINGS
by
ADRIAN VAN DIEST

This catalogue records Adrian van Diest's harbour and coastal scenes, in which a ship or ships are a major part of the scenery. It also records his naval battle scenes and his rare marine pictures.

The very large number of his landscapes are not recorded here; for those who are interested, the Witt Library in London holds a large archive of them. This catalogue is by no means complete, but represents pictures which are available for study.

Capriccio Harbour and Coastal Scenes

1. Coastal scene. Ferry boat, with figures, castle and hills right and left, ships beyond. Canvas. 40in. x 50¼in. Signed A. Van Diest. Sotheby's 30.10.91, Lot 120.

2. Coastal scene, with galley, English ship, castle and many figures and cows. Canvas. 25in. x 48in. Not signed. Christie's 24.10.74, Lot 87.

3. Estuary scene, with galley and English ship. Numerous figures and cows. Canvas. 30in. x 51in. Signed.

4. Large harbour scene, with galley and English warship. Elegant figures. Canvas. 43in. x 59in. Signed. Christie's 24.5.85, Lot 87.   *See Colour Plate 27*

5. Southern harbour with galley and ship. Canvas. 36¼in. x 59½in. Signed. Witt Library.

6. Long narrow (over-door) picture of sailing boats off the coast. Canvas. 13½in. x 42½in. Signed. Witt Library.

7. Long narrow (over-door) scene, coastal with a galley. Canvas. 15in. x 43in. Not signed (but very typical). Witt Library.

8. Very good picture of English ship at sea off a coastline. Canvas. 29½in. x 24½in. Signed A.V.D. Sotheby's 18.3.81, Lot 8.

9. An inlet with traders on a beach and a large English ship. Canvas. 67¾in. x 48¾in. At Kedelston Hall.

10. A picture very similar to No. 9 but with camels on shore. Canvas. 50in. x 60¼in. Signed. At Kedelston Hall.

11. An extensive coastal scene with small town on left, English ships and mountain on right. Canvas. 20¼in. x 29½in. Signed. A very beautiful picture. Witt Library.

12. An extensive coastal harbour scene with English ships and a castle on a little island. Canvas. 38in. x 67in. Private Collection.

13. Small, rather simple, harbour scene with British ship and large figures of men and girls in foreground. Canvas. Private Collection.   *See Colour Plate 28*

Pictures of Individual Ships, Marine Scenes and Battle Scenes

14. Fishing boats in a choppy sea, no land. Panel. 14in. x 18½in. Ex Ingram Collection. Witt Library.

15. English two-decker at sea, with lugger in foreground. Canvas. 15½in. x 18½in. Signed. Phillips 2.7.91, Lot 1. A most competent and attractive picture.

See Colour Plate 29

16. An English two-decker (firing a salute), starboard stern view, and another two-decker on right, broadside view. Two small typical figures in bottom right corner hauling nets. Canvas. 19in. x 24in. Not signed (but very typical). Christie's 7.10.93, Lot 406.

See Colour Plate 31

17. English two-decker at sea, calm, with lugger and large rock on right. Canvas. About 19in. x 24in. Signed A.V.D. Christie's 1977, Lot 169. *See Plate 15*

18. The *Mary Rose* action on 9 December 1669. Seven Algerine pirate ships were held off and defeated by the *Mary Rose* and her two escorts. Large canvas. 43¾in. x 71½in. Signed A.V.D. on back of canvas. Was with Leger Galleries. This is a copy of a Van de Velde in the Royal Collection. There is a mezzotint of this after Van de Velde engraved by Kirkall, and there is also an etching of this action engraved by W. Hollar. Hollar was himself aboard the *Mary Rose* during this action. *See Plate 16*

19. The Battle of Bantry Bay, 1 May 1689. Canvas. 37in. x 54in. Not signed. At N.M.M. *See Colour Plate 33*

20. A smaller version of No. 19. Canvas. 30in. x 25in. Sotheby's October 1972, Lot 165. Was with Richard Green Gallery.

21. Battle of La Hogue, 23 May 1692, showing blazing French ships driven ashore. Canvas. 35½in. x 44in. Signed. At N.M.M. *See Colour Plate 32*

22. Destruction of the *Soleil Royal* at the Battle of La Hogue, 23 May 1692. Large canvas. 36in. x 59½in. Signed. At N.M.M.

23. Action between an English 70 gun ship and two French privateers. Canvas. Not signed. Was with Parker Gallery. Now in private ownership.

24. Another battle off Cape Barfleur. Large canvas. Was with Simon Carter Gallery. N.M.M. photographic files.

Colour Plate 34. *Portrait of the* Royal Sovereign *of 1701. Note the extremely accurate and detailed painting, illustrated particularly by the magnified photographs in Colour Plates 35 and 36 (see also Frontispiece and page 5). The cool palette and numerous vessels on the horizon are typical. Catalogue No. 1.* PRIVATE COLLECTION

Chapter 5
L. d. MAN
fl. circa 1707–1725

L. d. Man has only recently emerged as a recognisable figure in early marine painting. The first step in the study of an undocumented painter like this is the collection of a basic body of work which can definitely be assigned to him, either because it is signed or because it has some outstanding style or idiosyncrasy.

During the past twenty-six years the author has found twenty-four examples of his work. Of these eight are clearly signed with his little crabbed signature –

Colour Plate 35. *Magnified view of the stern of the* Royal Sovereign *(Colour Plate 34) to show the detailed and lovingly rendered stern decoration.* PRIVATE COLLECTION

Colour Plate 36. *Magnified view of part of the rigging of the* Royal Sovereign *(Colour Plate 34) showing the typical careful drawing of the numerous small figures all doing something appropriate and all wearing little hats!* PRIVATE COLLECTION

L. d. Man – often right down on the bottom right or left of a picture, where it might normally be lost (or sometimes preserved!) under the rebate of a frame.

As the pictures gradually accumulated over the years certain facts about the artist became apparent.

Clearly, here was a highly individual talent. Neither his palette nor his style owed anything to the Van de Velde studio. (Many of the artists of this period continued to produce versions or often outright copies of Van de Velde subjects, painted in the same style and with the same warm palette of this school.) L. d. Man's subjects were painted in a cool, hard palette in which steely blue seas and grey and pink clouds predominated, quite different from the palette of the Van de Veldes and P. Monamy. It became increasingly obvious that this painter was Dutch and had learned his trade in Holland. His accurate, detailed and often rather formal way of painting his ships was very reminiscent of Abraham Storck and his school. They are painted in a very solid 'chunky' manner, usually sitting well down in the water (see Colour Plates 34 and 38).

Three of the twenty-four pictures found were Dutch scenes and the ships depicted were Dutch (Catalogue Nos. 3, 6 and 7). In fact, two of these pictures which were sold at auction in London were catalogued as by

Abraham Storck (No. 3) or by Jan Storck (No. 6). A third picture seen fleetingly in New York by the author was being sold as L. Backhuysen!

The rest of his pictures were nearly all English ship portraits, often of easily identifiable first-rates, such as the *Royal Sovereign* of 1701 (four pictures). Many more were of the royal yachts in service between 1700 and about 1720. In particular, the large three-masted ship-rigged yacht the *Royal Caroline* was a favourite subject for his brush (six pictures). All these ships are painted in accurate detail, very competently, and are very attractive and colourful ship portraits.

Characteristics of his Paintings

There is good perspective; it is characteristic of his pictures that the distance and horizon are often dotted with small ships gradually fading away into the background – all with excellent perspective (see Colour Plates 34, 37 and 38).

There are several further characteristic features of his paintings:

Depiction of Carving and Gilding
A major recognition feature of his works is the great attention to detail in the decorative carving and gilding round the bows, sterns and gunports of the ships. I know of no other artist of this period who spends so much labour on lovingly depicting all this decoration. Isaac Sailmaker, it is true, also spends much labour in this direction but in a different, less accurate and less sophisticated way. This feature is particularly shown in d. Man's paintings of the *Royal Sovereign* of 1701 (Colour Plate 35). This ship was decorated, gilded and carved so profusely and so much money was spent on this that she became something of a scandal in her own lifetime. L. d. Man's portraits of her illustrate this with great clarity. In fact, after this ship was launched the Admiralty put a moratorium on excessive decoration of ships, and many carvers and gilders were paid off and had to find other jobs ashore (such as church decoration and carving). This noticeable characteristic of L. d. Man's painting makes one wonder whether he himself was one of the army of gilders and artists originally employed in decorating the King's ships and yachts.

Figures
The second characteristic is that all his vessels are filled with many active little figures, all extremely

Plate 17. Magnified view of the signature on the picture shown in Colour Plate 39. It is always very small and low down either in the extreme right- or left-hand corner. All eight signatures found are similar to this one.

Plate 18. *A royal yacht (possibly the* Katherine*) in an estuary, with a Dutch town in the background (possibly Dordrecht). Signed. Note all the crew in tricorn hats again! Catalogue No. 6.*

well painted, in various attitudes and performing various tasks around the ship (Colour Plate 36 and Plate 18). Moreover, nearly all the figures are depicted wearing little black tricorn hats, even figures climbing the rigging, or furling sails! This seems to confirm the observation of Peter the Great of Russia who was visiting the shipyards of Britain during the later part of William III's reign (1698). He was most struck by the fact that everybody from the highest to the lowest wore hats, at all times, and he made a comment about this in his diary! This, also, is of some significance in the dating of L. d. Man's pictures.

Flags

The flags flown by ships painted in the first few years of the eighteenth century give an important clue to dating the work. Most ships of this era flew a red ensign at the stern. Prior to 1707 the ensign had a plain red St. George's cross on a white ground in the 'fly' (i.e. top left-hand corner of the flag). In 1707 this plain St. George's cross was replaced by the 'Union' (i.e. the combination of the red St. George's cross on the white St.

Colour Plate 37. *Portrait of the* Royal Caroline (ex Peregrine) *coming to anchor. This picture shows very well the cool palette, pink clouds, vessels on the horizon and great detail in the drawing of the yacht which is sitting well down in the water. Nearly all the typical characteristics of an L. d. Man painting are present here. Catalogue No. 7a.*

CHRISTIE'S

Colour Plate 38. *The royal yacht* Katherine *in a calm sea, firing a salute. An attractive small ship portrait. Catalogue No. 2a.* PRIVATE COLLECTION

Colour Plate 39. *The Royal Caroline and accompanying yachts, at sea in a gale. This is a typical 'rough sea painting', showing his rather formal depiction of the waves in fairly parallel lines. Catalogue No. 2.*
PRIVATE COLLECTION

Andrew's cross of Scotland). This means that paintings showing ships with the red ensign with the 'Union' in the fly must have been painted *after* 1707. All of L. d. Man's English paintings show ships with the Union in the fly, which means that he must have been painting them after 1707.

One further characteristic of this painter is that he paints a flag which is fluttering in a strong wind with a number of vertical parallel 'wrinkles'. This is highly typical and occurs in a number of his paintings (Colour Plates 39 and 41 and Plate 19).

His Painting of the Sea

His calm seas are a typical steely blue and look very good. His rougher seas are not as good as those of Van de Velde, being rather formalised as a series of parallel waves (Colour Plate 39). One is forced to the conclusion that he did not have much practical experience of rough seas!

So, taking all these idiosyncrasies together and looking at the main body of his work, we have a very recognisable painter, easily differentiated from the other marine painters of his age.

Moreover, about two-thirds of his known English works are of royal yachts or large prestigious English first-rates (such as the *Royal Sovereign*). During the whole of this period (1707 to about 1720) these ships spent the greater part of their time moored in the Thames near Deptford naval dockyard. It is tempting to postulate that it was at Deptford where many of these paintings were done.

What deductions can be made about our mysterious L. d. Man on the basis of this body of his work which we have just reviewed?

All eight of his signed paintings are signed in exactly the same way – L. d. Man. De Man is a Dutch or Flemish name. There was a large family of De Mans in Delft, and the well-known Dutch painter Cornelius de Man (1621-1706) belongs to this family. When signing his paintings Cornelius de Man signed C. d. Man, thus dropping the 'e' from the 'de' in exactly the same way as our painter L. d. Man does.

In an excellent and very long article on Cornelius de Man (C. Briere-Misme – *Oud Holland* 52. 1935) reference is made to his typical 'cool palette'. This is, as we have seen, a very good description of our painter's palette too. In this same article a fairly extensive review of Cornelius de Man's family is given, but unfortunately there is no reference here to an L. d. Man. In fact, although he had two married sisters, he is recorded as having died without children or close relatives.

Plate 19. *Dutch warship in a rough sea. Signed. Note the regular waves and the parallel folds of the flag, both typical of this artist. Catalogue No. 4.* PHILLIPS

As we have seen, the evidence from his paintings all points to his having been trained in the Dutch method of painting and three of his known marine paintings are entirely Dutch. One of them (Plate 18) shows a town in the background which is probably Dordrecht.

He must have done a good deal of his work at Deptford, as most of the royal yachts and large first-rates, such as the *Royal Sovereign,* were moored there at this period. However, an extensive search of the records of Dockyard employees and of crews of royal yachts of the period, which are held at the Record Office at Kew (all in great detail) have yielded no information. The same is true of contemporary Deptford Parish Registers and records of the two Dutch Reformed churches in London. There was a Dutch Reformed church on Canvey Island at this time but unfortunately all its records have been lost. Nor does his name appear among the naturalisation papers of the period (also held at Kew).

He appears to have worked independently, rather cut off from the mainstream of other artists of the time. There is no record of him at the Painter Stainers Company, or in any of the early art reference books (i.e. Walpole[1] and Edward Edwards[2]).

1. H. Walpole, *Anecdotes of Painting in England,* 5 vols., 1762-1771.
2. E. Edwards, *Anecdotes of Painters who have resided in, or been born in England,* London, 1808.

Colour Plate 40. *Dutch craft in a quiet estuary in Holland. This picture, which is signed, derives directly from the great tradition of sea and river painting of the inland waterways of Holland, by such artists as van Goyen, van Ruysdael and the later masters such as Abraham Storck and Aernout Smit etc. It could well have been painted by L. d. Man in Holland before he arrived in this country. A most attractive picture. Catalogue No. 3.* PRIVATE COLLECTION

From the evidence before us, therefore, we can make the following deductions:

1. He was Dutch and must have had some professional training under one of the established artists of the time. Either Abraham Storck or, possibly, L. Backhuysen spring to mind as his likely tutors. Both these masters had large 'schools' of pupils – not always fully documented. He probably painted some seascapes in Holland before he arrived in England.

2. He must have been working in England over the period 1707-1720 (approximately) and he must have been working at, or near, Deptford on the Thames, where nearly all the ships that he so faithfully portrayed were based.

3. The timing of his arrival in England, just about at the death of Van de Velde the Younger, suggests that he had little or no contact with the Van de

Colour Plate 41. *The* Royal Caroline *at sea. Note the typical vertical folds in the flag.* Catalogue No. 1a. PRIVATE COLLECTION

Velde studio – even that part of it which continued after the master's death. All his paintings are highly individual in style, composition and palette, and there is no evidence that he copied Van de Velde subjects, which nearly all the other early marine artists, except he and Sailmaker, did.

4. It is tempting to postulate that he was a minor member of the large de Man family of Delft. There was an artistic background to this family, with two well-established artists (Cornelius de Man and Cornelius Stangeris) and also a connection with the goldsmith's trade. But the evidence for this is, of course, very circumstantial and must await further research.

There must be many more of his paintings tucked away in old houses, lofts and collections in England, judging by the regularity with which they suddenly appear in the London salerooms.

Although no Van de Velde, he was a very competent, accurate and pleasing recorder of the beautifully decorated yachts and capital ships inhabiting the lower reaches of the Thames in the early years of the eighteenth century.

CATALOGUE OF PAINTINGS
by
L. d. MAN
(as known up to 1994)

The Catalogue is in two categories:

1. Undoubted signed examples
2. Very typical works, assigned with a high degree of certainty, but unsigned (shown with suffix a)

Category 1
Signed Examples

1. The *Royal Sovereign* of 1701 (stern and starboard view) with a galiot and another large warship, calm sea. 23in. x 28in. Signed lower left. Painted in great detail. Private Collection.   *See Colour Plate 34*

2. The *Royal Caroline* with another yacht, at sea in a swell. 23in. x 28in. Signed lower left. Sotheby's 29.1.64, Lot 71. Well painted in great detail. Private Collection.
See Colour Plate 39

3. A calm scene with a large galiot centre and warships right and left. Panel. 14in. x 19in. Signed lower right. Very attractive Dutch scene (with Dutch flags). Private Collection.
See Colour Plate 40

4. Small man-of-war, in rough seas off a rocky coast, stern and portside view. Panel. 15in. x 19in. Signed. Phillips 1980, Lot 38, to Ackermann. Well painted – great detail.
See Plate 19

5. The *Royal Sovereign,* coming to anchor in a calm, seen from port quarter, stern view. Canvas. 32in. x 36½in. Signed. Christie's 19.11.82, Lot 55.

6. A royal yacht (possibly the *Katherine)* with other small ships, port bow view. A Dutch town, probably Dordrecht, as background. Canvas. Signed. Christie's 16.5.75, Lot 163 (catalogued as Jan Storck).   *See Plate 18*

7. Two smalschips (Dutch) coming into port, rough sea. Panel. 10in. x 15¼in. Signed. At Ronald Cook Gallery, New Bond Street.

8. Stern quarter view of the *Royal Caroline* with many other yachts and shipping towards the horizon, a porpoise fin in the foreground. Signed. N.M.M. photographic files.

Category 2
Paintings not signed
but which are assigned to L. d. Man with a high degree of certainty

1a. Yacht *Royal Caroline* fully rigged at sea, seen broadside on with two other smaller yachts. Canvas. 14½in. x 20in. A moderate sea, well painted, good condition. Was in collection of Dr. Grace Simpson. Private Collection.   *See Colour Plate 41*

2a. Portrait of the royal yacht *Katherine,* port quarter view, many smaller ships around and on horizon, calm. Panel. 7½in. x 11in. Private Collection.   *See Colour Plate 38*

3a. Portrait of *Royal Caroline,* port quarter view, many other vessels around, calm. Panel. 11in. x 16in. Ex Caird Collection. Now in N.M.M.

4a. Portrait of *Royal Caroline,* port quarter view. Panel. 11in. x 16in. (This is exactly the same as No. 3a above, but with fewer background ships.) Private collection.

5a. Portrait of a royal yacht (possibly the *Mary),* port quarter view. Canvas. 23in. x 29½in. Ex McPherson Collection. Now in N.M.M.

6a. Two royal yachts, port quarter view, side by side, one ketch rigged (? *Fubbs),* the other smack rigged (? *Katherine).* Panel. 11in. x 16in. Ex Caird Collection. Now in N.M.M.

7a. Large portrait of *Royal Caroline* seen from port bow, coming to anchor, calm sea, small rowing boats in foreground, other ships on horizon. Canvas. 30in. x 28½in. Christie's 13.4.89, Lot 147 (£5,500). Very colourful and attractive picture.

See Colour Plate 37

8a. Two men-of-war (third-rates), one seen starboard quarter firing a salute, the other stern, starboard quarter. Calm, other ships and rowing boats in background. Panel. 10¾in. x 15¾in. Phillips 15.2.87, Lot 2 (catalogued as 'Circle of Peter Monamy').

9a. A smack-rigged yacht (possibly *Mary),* starboard view, calm, other vessels in background. Canvas. 33in. x 28in. Private Collection.

10a. Man-of-war (third-rate) plunging in a rough sea, seen from bows, port quarter. Canvas. 23in. x 28in. Private Collection.

11a. Marine view showing a royal yacht (probably *Fubbs)* in right foreground, other yachts and vessels to the left, calm, porpoises in foreground. Canvas. Fairly large painting. At present owned by New York Historical Society, 120 Central Park W., New York 10024.

12a. Two large men-of-war, stern views, in a calm sea, many smaller vessels towards the horizon. Canvas? Fairly large painting. N.M.M. photographic files.

13a. Two ships in a stormy sea, with black clouds. Dimensions not known. Very similar in style to No. 4 in this catalogue. N.M.M. photographic files.

14a. A smack-rigged yacht at sea with Dutch flag flying from jackstaff on bowsprit, full sails, seen from port quarter, other ships in background. Canvas? Large picture, 37in. x 52in. Was in possession of Cyril Andrade (dealer) in 1937. N.M.M. photographic files.

15a. Large view of several first-rate men-of-war in a calm estuary. Canvas. 29in. x 40in. Well painted attractive picture. Private collection N.M.M. photographic files.

Colour Plate 42. *The Battle of Cape Passaro, 31 July 1718. Signed H. Vale. This battle was fought by the British (commanded by Admiral Byng) against the Spanish during the War of the Spanish Succession. The painting depicts the central point of the battle when H.M.S.* Kent *and H.M.S.* Superbe *engaged and captured the Spanish flagship* Real San Felipe *(shown flying the white 'Cross of Burgundy'). Catalogue H. Vale No. 3.* LANE FINE ART

Chapter 6
H. VALE AND R. VALE
fl. circa 1705–1730

During the first quarter of the eighteenth century (roughly 1705-1727) a number of marine paintings appeared signed by two men, R. Vale and H. Vale. It is presumed from the name that they must have been native born English, but there is an almost total lack of documentary information about them. It is not known whether they were brothers, father and son or in fact in any way related. Everything about them has had to be deduced from the appearance of signed examples of their work in salerooms, museums and private collections. These signed examples have been slow in appearing and at the present moment the author has only been able to trace nine of them. Four are signed by R. Vale (one is signed Richard Vale and dated 1719) and five are signed H. Vale (three of these are dated 1713, 1714 and 1727 respectively).

Archibald[1] states that the quality of those pictures signed by R. Vale is not

1. E.H.H. Archibald. *Dictionary of Sea Painters*. Antique Collectors' Club, 2nd Edition, 1989.

Colour Plate 43. *Portrait of a fifth-rate man-of-war in three positions. Signed and dated H. Vale 1727. An accurate and well painted and attractive picture. Catalogue H. Vale No. 5.* SOTHEBY'S

Colour Plate 44. *A Dutch fluyt and an English yacht off a headland with a small castle. Well painted and bright. Must be attributed to the Vales, probably H. Vale. Catalogue Unsigned No. 1.* BONHAMS

The Royall Katherine Command by John Earl of Mulgrave in the Second Dutch Warr.

Plate 20. *The* Royal Katherine, *built in 1664 by Christopher Pett at Woolwich. She was a second-rate mounting about 82-86 guns. She fought throughout the second and third Dutch wars and was finally broken up about 1698. This portrait of her is therefore one of the earliest attributed to H. Vale. (It would have been painted a little later, of course, as a copy of an earlier Van de Velde or Sailmaker portrait.) It is by any standard a fine early ship portrait. Catalogue H. Vale No. 1.*

NATIONAL MARITIME MUSEUM

up to that of those signed by H. Vale and the author would agree with this assessment. In fact the pictures signed by H. Vale which have turned up recently go further to substantiate this view, showing that H. Vale was an accurate and competent painter (Colour Plates 42 and 43). R. Vale appears to be less gifted and his ships and seas are more primitive (Colour Plates 47 and 48).

The palette of these painters is especially noteworthy, being harsh and highly coloured and used in a rather primitive way, especially in the case of R. Vale. There is quite a large body of unsigned marine paintings, which must have been done between 1707 and 1730, which do not seem to be either quite good enough or typical enough to be the work of any of the other major marine artists of the period. These often appear as 'School of Monamy or Swaine' in auction catalogues – rather to the detriment of

Plate 21. *The Relief of Barcelona in April 1706. Signed H. Vale and dated 1713. Catalogue H. Vale No. 2.* NATIONAL MARITIME MUSEUM

these named artists! It is likely that quite a large number of such pictures could be the work of one or other of the Vales.

A further study of their work raises the question as to whether they were employed as 'copyists'. There is a large Van de Velde painting which used to hang in the old Admiralty Board Room which has been a favoured subject for 'copyists'. There are at least three pictures which are copies of the left half of this painting, by a much rougher and harsher hand, and two known copies of the right half. The technique and palette of these copies strongly suggest the work of one of the Vales, probably R. Vale (see Colour Plate 46). There is also a rather good and competent painting of the *Royal Katherine* – assigned to H. Vale – which must have been done a good deal later than the date of construction of the ship herself, and could be a copy of a Sailmaker contemporary portrait or of a Van de Velde (Plate 20). A further and even less well painted copy of this picture is also known. A yet further copy of Isaac Sailmaker's *Britannia,* by a less sure hand (Catalogue Unsigned No. 7), is also known. There therefore exists the possibility that the Vales may have started their careers as copyists in either the tail end of the Van de Velde studio or in the last days of the Sailmaker studio (when this artist was quite old and rather busier than usual, owing to the death of the Van de Veldes), or probably in both.

One final clue to their pictures is that H. Vale appears to have been

Colour Plate 45. *A fleet at anchor off a headland with small castle. The colouring, general composition and the sky suggest R. Vale. The figures are quite good but rather 'spindly' and definitely too big for the ships on which they are depicted, a fault which is very typical of R. Vale. Catalogue Unsigned No. 2.* Private Collection

Colour Plate 46. *This is a copy of the left half of a large and well-known Van de Velde which used to hang in the old Admiralty Board Room, until it was damaged in the last World War. The somewhat 'harsh' colouring and primitive figures suggest that R. Vale was the copyist. Catalogue Unsigned No. 5.* Private Collection

Colour Plate 47. *The Streights Fleet off a Mediterranean coast. Signed and dated Richard Vale 1719. This definite Richard Vale painting gives a good idea of his harsh, rather 'chocolate box' colouring and rather poor composition and drawing of the ships. Compare Colour Plates 45 and 46 and note that once again the figures are disproportionately large for the ships on which they are portrayed. Catalogue R. Vale No. 1.* Bridgeman Art Library and Christie's

employed by the Byng family to record some of the battles and episodes in the early years of the war of the Spanish Succession (1702-1720). A picture in the family collection at Southill Park of 'The Relief of Barcelona' is certainly by H. Vale. Further pictures of 'The Attack on Alicante', 'The Capture of Gibraltar' and 'The Battle of Cape Passaro (1718)' (Colour Plate 42) all record events in the war of the Spanish Succession associated with the career of Admiral Byng.

Characteristics of the Paintings

From a careful study of their known pictures it is possible to build up a sort of recognition schedule for the pictures, which must be dated between about 1705 and 1730 (the latest dated painting by H. Vale is 1727).

Palette
The palette is distinctive – rather harsh, bright, unblended or unsoftened colours are used, and laid on rather thickly, especially in the case of R. Vale. This tends to give the painting a rather 'chocolate box' sort of appearance in many cases.

Drawing and Composition
If the drawing and make up of the picture strike one as rather primitive, and there are obvious mistakes of perspective, then this is probably R. Vale. If the general make up of the picture is more competent and professional – and often rather pleasing (Colour Plates 43 and 44) – then this is probably H. Vale, who is also, in general, much better at painting the sea.

Figures
One defect which they both share to some extent is in the painting of the figures. Members of the crew, on the deck of a ship or in a barge or rowing boat, are usually disproportionately large and are rather spindly and primitive. This is particularly evident in some of the works which are copies of Van de Velde (Colour Plate 46). It cannot be ruled out that in some pictures the two artists may have co-operated.

The Drawing of the Sea
The drawing of the sea, particularly of a ruffled sea with a thick line of white to mark out the small waves and ripples, is very typical. It is a feature of several of their pictures and contributes to the general 'primitive' feel of

their work. However, in some of the better, later pictures, attributed to H. Vale particularly, the sea is rendered quite well (see Colour Plates 43 and 44).

These two artists, therefore, fell rather below the standard of the others who were painting during this period; they certainly were below the standards of realism and accuracy in which the great Dutch artists of the late seventeenth century excelled. Nevertheless, they obviously found a market for their cheerful and colourful productions amongst a less discerning and less affluent group of buyers, and it is likely that their pictures will continue to turn up in salerooms for some considerable time.

Plate 22. *This picture is signed R.V. (for Richard Vale) and again gives some idea of his slightly lesser quality than H. Vale. Catalogue R. Vale No. 2.* National Maritime Museum

Colour Plate 48. *A bright but rather primitive little 'over-door' picture which can be assigned to Richard Vale. Catalogue Unsigned No. 4.* SOTHEBY'S

Colour Plate 49. *Fishing vessels transferring their catch to shore, near a background port with a castle and white cliff which appears to be Dover. (This background has been used in several other pictures by Vale.) The figures and bright palette are typical of R. Vale. Catalogue Unsigned No. 12.* BONHAMS

CATALOGUE OF PAINTINGS
by H. Vale and R. Vale

This catalogue begins with the known signed pictures by H. Vale and continues with the signed pictures of R. Vale. The third part records a number of pictures which have been assigned to one or other of the Vales on stylistic evidence.

1. A good portrait of the *Royal Katherine,* in two positions, with other shipping. Canvas. 50in. x 65in. There is a large cartouche in the sky which says 'The Royal Katherine Command^d. by John Earl of Mulgrave in the Second Dutch Warr'. (This is actually incorrect – it should be in the *third* Dutch War!) This is a good portrait, well painted and with realistic sea. It bears many similarities to Isaac Sailmaker's portrait of the *Royal Prince,* which is now at Trinity House, and could well be a later copy or version of a similar painting. A prime characteristic of this painting is the large number of long, curly pennons. At N.M.M. Assigned to H. Vale. *See Plate 20*

Signed Pictures by H. Vale

2. 'The Relief of Barcelona'. Canvas. 44in. x 71in. Signed H. Vale and dated 1713. This also bears a large cartouche in the sky, saying 'Barcelona, Releiv'd by Sr John Leake, Vice Admirall of the White and Commander in Chief of ye Confederate Fleet April ye 27th Anno 1706'. There are three pictures of 'The Relief of Barcelona' and one of 'The Attack on Alicante', all by H. Vale (only one signed). All are episodes in the history of the Byng family from the family collection at Southill Park. At N.M.M. *See Plate 21*

3. The Battle of Cape Passaro. Canvas. 28in. x 46in. Signed H. Vale. Sotheby's 1990, Lot 70, bought by Lane-Fox (dealer). The Battle of Cape Passaro was on 31 July 1718 between the English, commanded by Admiral Byng (later second Earl of Torrington) and the Spanish. Central is the Spanish flagship *Real San Felipe,* which was captured.
See Colour Plate 42

4. An English frigate in two positions. Canvas. Signed H. Vale and dated 1714. Phillips 26.11.79, Lot 109. Was with dealer Paul Mason in 1980. A good straightforward ship portrait, well done.

5. A fourth-rate man-of-war, in three positions. Canvas. 37in. x 61in. Signed H. Vale and dated 1727. A very good, well painted picture. *See Colour Plate 43*

Signed Pictures by R. Vale

1. Streights Fleet off Mediterranean coast. Canvas. 35½in. x 64½in. Signed Richard Vale and dated 1719. Christie's 21.5.84 (Elveden Hall sale), Lot 21. Post 1707 flags.
See Colour Plate 47

2. English men-of-war at sea. Left a large man-of-war flying royal standard, stern view, other fleet units on right. Canvas. 33in. x 57in. Signed R.V. for Richard Vale. N.M.M. photographic files. *See Plate 22*

3. Two rather primitive little panels: 1. a galley and a frigate at sea; 2. frigate at sea. Panel. 20in. x 24in. Signed R. Vale. Both pictures show a pre-1707 ensign. N.M.M. photographic files.

Unsigned Paintings, attributable to the Vales

1. A Dutch fluyt and an English yacht, with a rowing barge, off shore (with small castle). Canvas. Approximately 29in. x 18½in. Ex Author's Collection. Bonhams 14.8.86, Lot 291. Attributed to H. Vale (sold as 'Circle of P. Monamy'). A bright and well painted little picture. *See Colour Plate 44*

2. A fleet at anchor in an estuary, with a small castle (see also No. 1). Canvas. 28in. x 47in. Christie's 1.3.85, Lot 80. Attributed to H. Vale. A bright, attractive picture. Private Collection. *See Colour Plate 45*

3. A man-of-war off some cliffs, with a large castle. Canvas. 12½in. x 14½in. Christie's 1.3.85, Lot 81. A typical Vale, probably H. Vale.

4. A long 'over-door' picture of men-of-war and yachts at sea. Canvas. 18in. x 58in. Sotheby's 13.7.88, Lot 1. Attributed to Richard Vale. Typical Vale palette.

See Colour Plate 48

5. Copy of the left half of a large Van de Velde picture which was in the old Admiralty Board Room (Government Art Collection 4109, and described in detail by M.S. Robinson on page 958 of his catalogue of the Van de Veldes). The picture has been a favourite subject for copyists and at least eleven versions are known and are listed by Robinson. This version bears the typical Vale palette and the figures in the rowing boat are particularly typical of R. Vale. Ex Author's Collection. *See Colour Plate 46*

6. Portrait of the *Royal Katherine*. This is probably a version or copy of H. Vale's portrait (Catalogue No. 1), but by a very much less practised hand. It is also notable for its large display of curling pennons and it shows the broadside and stern view. Canvas. Very large picture. Possibly by R. Vale. It is owned by the N.M.M., on permanent loan to the Royal Naval College.

7. Portrait of the *Britannia,* part broadside view (rather similar to Isaac Sailmaker's portrait of the same ship and could be a copy or version of this painting). Stiff flags and no curling pennons. Attributed to R. Vale. Was with the Parker Gallery in 1969.

8. Another version of the Battle of Cape Passaro. Canvas. 25in. x 43in. Sotheby's November 1987, Lot 4 (attributed to Woodcock). Not so well painted as H. Vale's version and the sky particularly looks like R. Vale's palette.

9. Capture of Gibraltar 22 July 1704 by Admiral Rooke. Canvas. 27in. x 49in. Phillips 28.1.74. This must be an H. Vale.

10. An English man-of-war and other vessels off a coast with a large castle. Canvas. Approximately 39in. x 49¼in. Sotheby's 17.7.85, Lot 8. H. Vale? N.M.M. photographic files.

11. Man-of-war, running, in a stiff breeze. Canvas. 24½in. x 30½in. Christie's 16.10.87, Lot 65. H. Vale? N.M.M. photographic files.

12. Figures loading a fishing boat, with a town on the shore line, very colourful. Canvas. 12in. x 14in. Bonhams January 1986, Lot 88. R.Vale? *See Colour Plate 49*

13. Dutch East Indiaman and a yacht, with a town (? Portsmouth) beyond. Canvas. 12in. x 14in. Bonhams January 1986, Lot 87. H. Vale?

14. A British third-rate off a coastal harbour, during the Anglo-Spanish wars. Canvas. 25in. x 44in. Sotheby's 18.11.92, Lot 4. The typical method of painting the sea and the more restrained colours point to H. Vale as the artist.

Colour Plate 50. *Large painting of the* Sovereign of the Seas *(later called the* Royal Sovereign). *This painting at Parham Park, Sussex, is a copy of the earlier engraving by John Payne. Catalogue No. 1.*   PARHAM PARK, SUSSEX

Chapter 7
LORENZO A. CASTRO
fl. circa 1672-1686

Bénézit, the comprehensive reference book of painters and engravers through the centuries, mentions no fewer than thirty-six Castros! It is not surprising, therefore, that there has been some difficulty in the precise identification of this artist. It does seem certain, however, that he was of Portuguese-Jewish descent and that he lived and had his early training in Antwerp.

There was apparently a large and significant Portuguese 'Nation' in Antwerp in the seventeenth century, originating in the severe persecution of the Jews by the Inquisition in Portugal in the early 1600s. Amongst these were several with the family name of Castro.

A Laureys A. Castro was listed as Master of the St. Luke's Guild of Painters in Antwerp in 1664-65. One theory is that this was the L.A. Castro who later appeared in England as a painter of marines. However, there was also an earlier marine painter working with, and in the style of, Andries van Eertvelt, called Sebastian D. Castro. According to Thieme-Becker,[1] our Lorenzo A. Castro was probably his son, and this would at

1. Thieme, U. and Becker, F. *Allgemeines Lexikon der Bildenden Künstler von der Antike bis zur Gegenwart.* 37 vols. Leipzig 1907-1950.

Plate 23. *A galley of Malta. Catalogue No. 7.*   DULWICH PICTURE GALLERY

least explain his early training in marine painting. Whichever of these theories is correct, it is evident that young Lorenzo had an extensive acquaintance with Mediterranean ports, such as Genoa, Malta, Lisbon etc. He also must have had some first-hand knowledge of Mediterranean galleys, which obviously fascinated him, as a large part of his artistic output consists of capriccio scenes of southern ports with several galleys very accurately and beautifully drawn.

He appears to have either settled in England or visited our shores for long periods, as many of his works were sold on the English market or were commissioned in England. His earliest signed and dated work is 1672 (a fanciful picture of the Battle of Actium, now held at the National Maritime Museum, Greenwich – Catalogue No. 8). In 1680 he was commissioned to paint the portrait of Sir Robert Clayton (then Lord Mayor of London) and Lady Clayton (which is signed and dated 1680 – Catalogue Nos. 27 and 28). The portrait of Sir Robert is now at the Bank of England.

The Dulwich Picture Gallery has six pictures by Castro. These are the remains of a dozen or so seascapes which were collected by William Cartwright as part of the Cartwright Collection which he bought in England and bequeathed to Dulwich College in 1686, forming the nucleus of the present collection at the Dulwich Picture Gallery.[2]

These dates give a good clue to the period when Castro was working in England, namely between 1672 and 1686.

2. *Mr. Cartwright's Pictures.* Catalogue of Exhibition at Dulwich Picture Gallery, 25 November 1987.

98

Plate 24. A Dutch East Indiaman off the town of Hoorn, in Holland. Catalogue No. 3.

The Paintings

Twenty-nine pictures by Castro have been traced and studied. Their subjects are:

18 southern harbour scenes
1 Dutch harbour scene (shipping off Hoorn)
6 battle scenes at sea
1 large ship portrait *(Sovereign of the Seas)*
3 large portraits

Fourteen of these pictures are signed, either Castro or L. Castro or L.A. Castro being the form of the signature. From these signed pictures a good idea of the artist's palette, technique and general picture construction can

Plate 25. *A small English merchantman and caravels off a southern coastline. Catalogue No. 4.*
DULWICH PICTURE GALLERY

be formed, making the attribution of other unsigned pictures easier.

All except one of his harbour capriccio scenes are of Mediterranean ports with a stone landing stage and perhaps a few buildings, with a wall or tower to one side, and his ships and galleys in the centre and opposite side (see Plates 25 and 26). The general construction of the pictures is quite sophisticated with good use of perspective. In all of them typical Mediterranean galleys are prominent – extremely colourful and well painted (see Plate 23). The other noticeable thing is that the shore and small boats are peopled with large, excellently drawn figures. They are either in groups 'discussing business' or handling the casks or bales of cargo. The clothes of the 'merchants' are accurately shown often allowing one to date the picture by the clothes, or deduce in which country the scene is set.

There is only one picture (Plate 24) which can be recognised as possibly

Colour Plate 51. *A sea fight between an English ship and Barbary Corsairs. This could represent the* Kingfisher *action of May 1681 when Sir John Kempthorne beat off seven Barbary ships. Catalogue No. 2.*

DULWICH PICTURE GALLERY

a Dutch port, but there are no English ports. This is really rather extra-ordinary as most of them must have been painted in England for the English market (for example, the Cartwright pictures at the Dulwich Picture Gallery).

There must have been a steady demand for warm Mediterranean scenes – as we have already noted, Adrian van Diest also found a ready sale for his Mediterranean capriccios. One can only surmise that these warm southern scenes must have excited a feeling of wonder, adventure, and longing for the colourful sunny southern lands and harbours depicted. There is no doubt that he would have been a huge success illustrating a Spanish or Italian travel brochure in these modern times! Also, of course, in an age before photography they would have been wonderful mementos for those rare people who had actually travelled abroad and seen such scenes.

Once again it is perhaps not surprising that five of his six battle scenes are

Plate 26. A Dutch ship and three galleys in a southern harbour. Catalogue No. 9.

Plate 27. *A British squadron and several Levantine galleys in the Straits of Messina, Mount Etna in the background. Catalogue No. 18.*   SOTHEBY'S

sea fights in the Mediterranean between the Turkish Algerine Corsairs (easily identifiable by the Turkish flag, with the triple crescent) and ships of either the English, Dutch or Danes (Colour Plate 51 and Plate 28). The actions of the third Dutch war (1672-1674) which was probably in full swing when he first came to England did not bring forth a single picture by Castro.

However, from 1672-1686 (the period when he was probably working in England) the British maintained a permanent presence in the Mediterranean (called the Streights Fleet) to protect our merchant shipping from the Barbary Corsairs, mostly based at Algiers. During this time quite a number of skirmishes and actions took place, and it is natural that these would have interested Castro particularly. For instance, in the Dulwich Picture Gallery is a large canvas of a sea battle between a large English warship and several Algerine men-of-war (Colour Plate 51). This could well be the occasion in 1681 when the English ship *Kingfisher* was attacked by seven Barbary ships. Her captain, Sir John Kempthorne, drove them off in a long action but was killed himself during the fighting. Another sea battle painted by Castro was a rather fanciful one of the ancient Battle of Actium (31 BC) which is at the National Maritime Museum, Greenwich (Catalogue No. 8).

There is only one formal ship portrait by him (Colour Plate 50), but this is an enormous (54in. x 96in.) painting of the *Sovereign of the Seas* (now at Parham Park) which was built by Phineas and Peter Pett and launched in 1637.[3] This painting is in fact a detailed copy of the original engraving by one of the early 'line engravers' called John Payne, which was probably completed in about 1640. This ship, which was later called the *Royal Sovereign,* was the biggest of her time and the first to carry one hundred

3. E.H.H. Archibald. *Dictionary of Sea Painters*. Antique Collectors' Club, 2nd Edition, 1989.

Plate 28. *Maltese galleys attacking a Barbary Corsair ship. Catalogue No. 25.* Sotheby's

guns. She fought in many actions during the Dutch wars and had two major refits before being destroyed accidentally by a fire in 1696 (see Chapter 1).

In addition to his marine paintings, Castro was an accomplished portrait painter. His two most famous and well documented portraits are those of Sir Robert and Lady Clayton (signed and dated 1680). Sir Robert was Lord Mayor of London at this time and the portraits were at the Clayton's country house, Harleyford Manor on the Thames, until 1950 when they were sold at Christie's (23 June 1950, Lots 31 and 32). They were bought by a dealer and Sir Robert's portrait can now be seen at the Bank of England.

Some Characteristics of his Paintings

His work demonstrates that he was well trained, probably in his native Antwerp. The construction of the pictures is pleasing, with good use of perspective, although in some of his seascapes the canvas becomes a little overcrowded (Colour Plate 51). His palette is fairly restrained and the pictures do not appear over bright, as do some of the works of Jacob Knyff, for instance. As already mentioned, he was particularly good at painting the colourful Mediterranean galleys with their multicoloured awnings and some of the best representations of these 'nearly out of date' craft are found

Plate 29. *A southern port with a galley being loaded. Catalogue No. 15.* SOTHEBY'S

in his works (Plates 23 and 28).

Another major characteristic is his competent handling of the figures which appear on the quays to the right or left of many of his harbour scenes, rather reminiscent of the style of Abraham Storck (see Plate 29).

The paintings as a whole project a feeling that they are Continental, not English, in their style, in a somewhat indefinable manner.

I cannot help feeling that there must be quite a lot of his pictures floating around in odd corners of the world and in the less well-known salerooms!

CATALOGUE OF PAINTINGS
by
L.A. CASTRO

Signed or definitely attributable pictures are listed first.

1. *Sovereign of the Seas*. Ship portrait after the engraving by John Payne. Canvas. 54in. x 96in. Signed L.A. Castro. Note the large number of curling decorative pennons in the rigging. At Parham Park. *See Colour Plate 50*

2. A sea fight between an English ship and the Barbary Corsairs. Canvas. About 47⅛in. x 36½in. Signed. This possibly represents the *'Kingfisher* Action' in May 1681 when Sir John Kempthorne beat off seven Barbary ships. At the Dulwich Art Gallery. *See Colour Plate 51*

3. A sea piece, a Dutch East Indiaman off Hoorn. Canvas. About 25in. x 30in. Signed. At the Dulwich Art Gallery. *See Plate 24*

4. A small English armed merchantman and two small caravels, in calm water, with a quay and coastline with a tower to the right. Canvas. About 24¾in. x 30in. Signed. A most attractive little picture. At the Dulwich Art Gallery. *See Plate 25*

5. Ships in rough water off a Mediterranean port. Canvas. About 37½in. x 70in. Signed. A large, ambitious work, showing English and Dutch ships, plus the usual moored galley on the left. At the Dulwich Art Gallery.

6. Two Dutch merchant ships in a rough sea off a quay. Canvas. About 18½in. x 25⅛in. Signed. At the Dulwich Art Gallery.

7. A galley of Malta off a quay and a coastline. Canvas. About 30in. x 52¾in. Signed. A lovely accurate study of a Maltese galley, with a prominent Maltese cross on the flag. At the Dulwich Art Gallery. *See Plate 23*

8. The Battle of Actium (31 BC). Canvas. 45in. x 62in. Signed and dated 1672. A fanciful picture and Castro's earliest dated picture. At N.M.M.

9. A ship (on left) and three galleys in a harbour (on right). Canvas. 41in. x 70in. Signed. Christie's 28.6.74, Lot 13. *See Plate 26*

10. Dutch Levanters and other vessels in a ruffled sea off a southern port. Canvas. 45in. x 54in. Signed. Christie's 15.7.77, Lot 120. Was in the possession of Westbourne Fine Arts Ltd., London.

11. Capriccio harbour scene with a mansion, a large ship and galleys. Canvas. 31½in. x 61in. Signed. Christie's 23.6.50, Lot 33. Formerly in the collection of Sir Robert Clayton at Harleyford Manor. Bought by Carr.

12. Mediterranean galleys at sea off a coast. Canvas. 35in. x 59in. Signed. Christie's 7.12.25, Lot 61 (Goff Sale). Attractive picture, very typical. Witt Library.

13. A Dutch Levanter and other ships off a Portuguese or Spanish seaport with a prominent church with two tall towers. Canvas. 50in. x 82in. Signed. Private Collection. Witt Library.

14. A Genoese galley off a quay, with a column, and stone arch on right. Canvas. Signed. Ex MacPherson Collection. (Also referred to in Chatterton's *Old Sea Paintings.*) Witt Library.

15. A southern port with a galley being loaded, numerous large elegant figures on the quay. Canvas. 18in. x 23in. Sotheby's 14.12.77, Lot 169. Witt Library.   *See Plate 29*

16. Large British man-of-war and a galley in a southern port, with numerous figures. Canvas. 39in. x 49in. Signed. Christie's 8.11.52. Bought by Letscher. Witt Library.

17. Genoese galley in a southern harbour (another version of No. 14). Canvas. About 12in. x 24in. Signed. Originally in Author's Collection.

18. A British squadron and several Levantine galleys in the Straits of Messina. Canvas. 30in. x 64in. Not signed. Was at Admiralty House, owned by Lord Mountbatten. Sotheby's 9.12.92, Lot 134.   *See Plate 27*

19. Action between English and Barbary ships. 43in. x 64in. Not signed. Acquired by N.M.M. in 1942. Reserve Collection.

20. Another battle between English ships and Barbary Corsairs. Large size. Not signed? In possession of H.R.H. Prince Antoine de Ligne, Château de Boloeil, Belgium.

21. A sea battle between Barbary Corsairs and Danes. 32½in. x 43¼in. Not signed. Sotheby's 10.12.86, Lot 103.

22. Three men-of-war saluting (they appear Dutch). *(No* galleys – very curling pennons from mast-head.) 10¾in. x 19½. Not signed. N.M.M. photographic files.

23. Dutch men-of-war and a 'buss' in heavy seas. A pair to No. 22. 10¾in. x 19½in. Not signed. N.M.M. photographic files.

24. Ships off a fortress (which could be Malta). 13in. x 15in. Not signed. Sotheby's 8.7.87, Lot 199. Witt Library.

25. Galleys (Maltese?) attacking a Corsair ship. Canvas. Not signed. Sotheby's 1.4.92, Lot 93.   *See Plate 28*

26. An English East Indiaman and numerous small boats loading stores at possibly a Portuguese port. Canvas. 34in. x 64in. Not signed. Bonhams 7.12.79, Lot 32.

Portraits

27. Portrait of Lady Clayton. Canvas. 93in. x 57in. Signed and dated 1680. Christie's 23.6.50, Lot 31.

28. Portrait of Sir Robert Clayton. Canvas. 93in. x 57in. Signed. Christie's 23.6.50, Lot 32. (Sir Robert Clayton was Lord Mayor of London). Now at Bank of England.

29. A second smaller and earlier portrait of Lady Clayton. Witt Library.

Chapter 8

THE LATE
VAN DE VELDE STUDIO
1690-1707
and the two chief studio assistants
JOHAN C. VAN DER HAGEN
1645-circa 1720
and
CORNELIS VAN DE VELDE
1675-1729

The Van de Veldes, father and son, came to England in 1673, by invitation from Charles II. They started their studio at Greenwich. Van de Velde the Elder did mostly drawings and grisailles, with a few oil paintings as well. The son did a lot of drawings but specialised in oil paintings for which he soon became famous. His work was in such demand that during the last years of the studio (roughly 1690-1707) at least two studio assistants were employed. Although it is quite possible that A. van Diest and the young Peter Monamy may have found temporary work there, the two main studio assistants were Cornelis van de Velde and Johan van der Hagen.

Since the publication of Mr. M.S. Robinson's large and exhaustive book surveying the life work of the Van de Veldes,[1] it has become much more evident how the studio functioned during its last years. In fact it became a sort of marine painting factory, with Willem van de Velde the Younger drawing the outline and doing a variable degree of the actual painting, while the finishing off was done by the studio assistants. When a picture was particularly attractive and sought after, up to three or four copies or 'versions' would be 'run off' by the studio assistants with little or no contribution from the master. Thus M.S. Robinson repeatedly found that there were nearly always up to two or three versions of a given picture which had been identified as coming from the Van de Velde studio – and in some cases there were up to ten or more versions in existence. Many of these copies were done almost entirely by the two main studio assistants; they were sometimes signed on the back of the canvas by Van de Velde, and sometimes not.

During the 'Dutch period' of the Van de Veldes, father and son (roughly 1650-1673), the pictures were usually signed with the small printed type monogram W.V.V. – although there are occasional variations. However,

1. *The Paintings of the Willem Van de Veldes,* two volumes by M.S. Robinson, published by the Trustees of the National Maritime Museum, 1990.

Plate 30. Johan C. van der Hagen. *This picture is post 1707 (judging by the red ensign flying on the stern of both ships). It is signed I.V.H., very unobtrusively, on the rudder of the small ship in the right foreground (see Plate 31). Also note the typical low ships on the horizon. Catalogue No. 5.*

Plate 31. *The small, unobtrusive signature I.V.H. tucked away on the rudder of the lugger in the right foreground of Plate 30.*

during the 'English period' of the studio (roughly 1678-1707) the larger, flowing, so-called round signature appears more often. The appearance of a genuine signature on the front of the picture usually means that Willem van de Velde the Younger did at least a large part of the painting himself. During the later days of the studio he often signed his large flowing signature on the back of the canvas, but this did not necessarily mean that he had done all the painting himself, simply that it was an 'approved' studio production.

When Van de Velde the Younger died in 1707 the studio continued to produce 'Van de Veldes' for a short time (Colour Plate 52) and then Cornelis van de Velde and J. van der Hagen began to produce their own individual pictures, which they started to sign in their own names. Cornelis van de Velde acquired a considerable reputation before his own death in 1729 and Van der Hagen also started painting his own pictures and signing them, although he did not acquire such a wide reputation as Cornelis.

Thus during the years following 1707, these two gentlemen produced, and sometimes signed, pictures of their own composition, but, as they had both trained and worked extensively in the Van de Velde studio, these later pictures all looked very much like late Van de Velde studio productions. This is the cause of much trouble in recognition and identification, especially if unsigned.

In order to try to sort out this confusion to some extent, this assessment of the two artists is based mainly on signed pictures, most of which were therefore done after 1707, when their master died. When it is present in a picture, the post 1707 red ensign (i.e. an ensign with *both the St. George's and the white St. Andrew's cross* in the fly) is a great help in dating the picture – and thus indirectly indicating one of these two painters as the probable artist. Just to make things more difficult, however, both of them are known to have produced straight copies of pre-1707 Van de Velde compositions *after* his death! Colour Plate 52 is a possible example. A perusal of M.S. Robinson's comments on the numerous copies of certain Van de Velde compositions shows how difficult this problem can be even in the hands of recognised experts (see Colour Plate 54).

However, the importance of a correct assignment to this or that artist has been rather over-emphasised recently, particularly in the assessment of the value of one of these pictures. After all, the worth of such a picture must to a large extent stand on its own true artistic and historical merit. An attractive, correct and well painted picture must have been done by a good, well trained and experienced artist of this group, even if he can only be tentatively identified.

*Plate 32. **Johan C. van der Hagen.** For comparison with Plate 30. This unsigned picture shows many Van der Hagen characteristics such as the low, long hulls on the horizon and the over-long bowsprit of the Dutch ship on the left.*

Johan C. van der Hagen
1645– circa 1720

There were at least two Van der Hagens working in the early eighteenth century.

Willem van der Hagen, whose exact dates are not known, seems to have worked mainly in Ireland, in the first half of the eighteenth century. There is a view of Waterford by him, signed and dated 1736. He was not primarily a marine painter, but seems to have specialised in landscapes and particularly 'harbour-scapes', where ships are secondary to the main theme. In the National Maritime Museum's photographic files there are fourteen pictures attributed to him. Subjects include Guernsey, Gibraltar (three), Messina, Falmouth and Plymouth. There is also a painting of William III landing at Carrickfergus – fully signed (Plate 36).

Plate 33. Johan C. van der Hagen. *A Dutch yacht and a small Boeier yacht and other shipping off a coast. Signed on the spar sticking out of the water. An intimate little Dutch scene. Catalogue No. 6.*

Plate 34. Johan C. van der Hagen. *One of his more common storm scenes with menacing rocks too close for safety. Signed I.V.H. on the spar in the water near the rock. Such scenes were very popular in the seventeenth century. Catalogue No. 7.*
CHRISTIE'S

Plate 35. Johan C. van der Hagen. A Dutch Kaag at sea. Note the typical long, low ship on the horizon and the 'out of true' bowsprit, two characteristics of Van der Hagen.
PRIVATE COLLECTION

Willem may have been related to our J.C. van der Hagen,[2] who was born in The Hague in 1645 and died in about 1720. Except for this, very little is known of Johan's life. He was almost certainly of the same family as a well-known seventeenth century Dutch landscape painter called Joris van der Hagen (1615-1669) who died in The Hague where our Johan van der Hagen was born.

Although there is no documentary evidence, it seems almost certain that when he came to England at the end of the seventeenth century he joined the studio of Willem van de Velde the Younger, as a regular studio assistant; there he absorbed the typical Van de Velde technique and palette.

2. 'The Willem Van de Veldes, Fred Cook Memorial Lecture', by E.H.H. Archibald, *Proceedings of the Royal Society of Arts*, 1982.

113

Colour Plate 52. Johan C. van der Hagen. *An Admiralty yacht at sea. Note the long bowsprit sticking up at the wrong angle! This must have been done around 1707 because it shows the pre-1707 red ensign. It is not signed and is probably a version of a Van de Velde composition done mostly by Van der Hagen. The brownish colour of the sea is very typical of the late Van de Velde studio productions.* PRIVATE COLLECTION

Plate 36. Willem van der Hagen. This is a scene of King William III landing at Carrickfergus (1690). It is signed by W. van der Hagen (working in Ireland). Note the artificial looking sea and the rather stiff painting of the main ship.
NATIONAL MARITIME MUSEUM

Characteristics of his Paintings

He was (according to Vertue[3]) 'an indifferent Dutch painter' but he certainly had some recognisable habits in his paintings of ships at sea. These were:

1. A tendency to get the bowsprit too long and sticking up at the wrong angle (Plates 30, 32, 35 and Colour Plate 52).
2. The horizon is often occupied by several ships, sketchily drawn and long and low in the water (Plates 30, 32 and 35).
3. He tended to specialise in rough seas, with numerous white flecks of rather frothy foam.

3. G. Vertue. Notebooks, 6 vols., 1715-1754. Published by the Walpole Society, Oxford.

115

Plate 37. Willem van der Hagen. Another more typical W. van der Hagen, of Gibraltar. Signed and dated 1722. NATIONAL MARITIME MUSEUM

4. His signature was often small and inconspicuous, hidden somewhere in the lower half of the picture. Often he signed just I.V.H. (see Plate 31).

Apart from these characteristics, his palette was of a brownish hue and his general composition was similar to that of the Van de Velde studio.

CATALOGUE OF *SIGNED* WORKS
BY
JOHAN C. VAN DER HAGEN

1. English ships in a storm. Canvas. 37½in. x 50in. Signed and dated 1714. Sotheby's 28.1.3, Lot 45. Now at N.M.M.

2. A ketch-rigged royal yacht in a stiff breeze. Canvas. 18in. x 16in. Signed. Was with Spink & Sons in 1959. Now at N.M.M.

3. An English ship driving on to the rocks. Canvas. 10½in. x 15¼in. Signed. At N.M.M.

4. The sunset gun, a fleet at anchor in a calm. Canvas. 35in. x 49in. Signed. Private Collection. Witt Library.

5. Two coastal merchantmen and a small lugger in a fair breeze. Canvas. About 30in. x 34in. Signed I.V.H. Private Collection. *See Plate 30*

6. Small Dutch ships at sea, off a coastline. Canvas. About 20in. x 24in. Signed. Was with Rupert Preston in 1975. *See Plate 33*

7. A partly dismasted frigate in heavy seas off a rocky shore. Canvas. 17in. x 24in. Signed I.V.H. Christie's 1.11.91, Lot 140. *See Plate 34*

Plate 38. Cornelis van de Velde. A masterly piece of painting, done from a typical 'Van de Velde' original but nevertheless a fine painting by Cornelis van de Velde, probably executed about 1707. Signed, lower right, C.V. Velde. Catalogue No. 1. SOTHEBY'S

Cornelis van de Velde
1675-1729

Cornelis was the son of Willem van de Velde the Younger, born in England after the family moved from Holland. He married Bernada, daughter of J.C. van der Hagen, in 1699. He was trained and brought up in the environs of his father's studio and during the last ten years or so of his father's life he was the main studio assistant. He seems to have absorbed his father's style and palette so completely that it is often difficult to be certain who actually did most of the painting of a late 'Van de Velde studio' production. Many of the late studio pictures of which several copies or 'studio versions' have been done are probably very largely by Cornelis.

After 1707, when his father died, Cornelis continued to turn out these studio Van de Veldes for some time. It is believed that he started to sign some of these pictures with his own name at this time – although while working as his father's assistant he probably did not sign his own name.

Characteristics of his Paintings

From the few existing signed pictures by him it is possible to gather some inkling of his personal style. Perhaps his main characteristic was that his painting was bolder and his lines heavier than his father's. For instance, the rigging lines in his pictures are thicker and bolder than those of a classic Van de Velde. He also seems to have excelled at storm scenes (see Plates 38 and 39).

Colour Plate 53. Cornelis van de Velde. A picture from the late Van de Velde studio period (1707 or near this date) which shows a large royal yacht (possibly the Mary*) signalling by gunfire and 'shaking the sails'. This was an accepted signal of the period for 'Enemy in sight'. It has been accepted that this is mainly, if not entirely, by Cornelis van de Velde, after a design by the master. The rather regular waves of the rough sea and the slope of the bowsprit which is somewhat out of true are both characteristics of Cornelis (see Robinson,* The Paintings of the Willem Van de Veldes, *Vol. II, p. 1003).*   BRIDGEMAN ART LIBRARY AND ALAN JACOBS GALLERY, LONDON

It is interesting that, unlike Van der Hagen, no *signed* picture has yet turned up with a ship wearing the post 1707 red ensign. This suggests that for a considerable time after his father's death in 1707 he really only continued to create further versions of his father's pictures (see Colour Plate 54).

Thus, although he continued the studio after 1707, he never developed a really recognisable artistic personality of his own. A browse through the numerous illustrations and descriptions of the Van de Velde works in M.S. Robinson's monumental work brings one inevitably to this conclusion. In spite of all this he seems to have acquired a considerable reputation in his own lifetime. For instance, he was asked to report on the progress of Sir James Thornhill's work in the Painted Hall at Greenwich in 1717.

The whole scene is complicated further by the fact that by 1720 the young Peter Monamy was turning out pictures which were very close imitations of Van de Velde subjects and not necessarily signing them. The same can also be said of the young Charles Brooking and the young John Clevely. The marine picture buying public in England still wanted 'Van de Veldes' and all these young artists began by supplying this demand. Even if they originally signed their pictures unscrupulous dealers sometimes are known to have erased the signature!

Colour Plate 54. This painting was a very popular late Van de Velde studio piece, of which there are no fewer than six contemporary versions. The one shown here is No. 5 in Robinson's The Paintings of the Willem Van de Veldes *(page 1058). It is unsigned but has all the characteristics of a Cornelis Van de Velde. It may even have been done just* after *Willem's death in 1707. It is included here to illustrate just how difficult it is to allocate the authorship of a 'Van de Velde studio' painting of this period.*   PRIVATE COLLECTION

    In this connection the following story about Charles Brooking, which occurs in Edward Edwards' *Anecdotes of Painters,* 1808, is worth repeating. Brooking would seem to have fallen into the hands of such a dealer for, as Edwards reports, Brooking

    painted much for a person who lived in Castle St. Leicester Square not far from the Mews … who coloured prints and dealt in pictures, which he exposed at his shop window. Brooking was accustomed to write his name upon his pictures, which mark was constantly obliterated by the shop-keeper before he placed them in his window … A gentleman who sometimes passed the shop, being struck with the merits of some sea-pieces, which were by the hand of this artist desired to know his name; but his enquiries were not answered agreeably to his wishes; he was only told that if he pleased they would produce any that he might require from the same painter … it however happened that the artist carried home a piece, on which his name was inscribed, while the master was not at home; and the wife who received it, placed it in the window without effacing the signature. Luckily, the gentleman passed by before the

Plate 39. Cornelis van de Velde. *This is the only signed and dated picture by Cornelis van de Velde that is known. It is dated 1707. Note the 'curly foam' on the tops of the waves and the rather heavy painting of the rigging, both characteristics of this painter. Catalogue No. 2.*
PRIVATE COLLECTION

picture was removed, and discovered the name of the painter whose work he so justly admired. He immediately advertised for the artist to meet him at a certain linen drapers in the city. To this invitation Brooking at first paid no regard; but seeing it repeated with assurances of benefit to the person to whom it was addressed, he prudently attended and had an interview with the gentleman, who from that time became his friend and patron.

CATALOGUE OF *SIGNED* PICTURES
BY
CORNELIS VAN DE VELDE

1. An English ship in a gale, trying to claw off a lee coast. Canvas. 24¾in. x 42in. Signed lower right C.V. Velde. Sotheby's 9.7.86, Lot 3. Was in the possession of T. Agnew & Sons.

See Plate 38

2. English ships at sea in a gale under low canvas. Canvas. 46½in. x 40in. Signed C.V. Velde (on back of original canvas) and dated 1707. Was with David Carrit, London, in 1980.

See Plate 39

3. English ships at sea, beating against a gale. Canvas. Probably 46in. x 40in. Signed C.V. Velde on back of canvas. Private Collection.

4. English yachts in a calm, one firing a salute. Canvas. 36in. x 55in. Signed C.V. Velde. In possession of Rupert Preston Gallery in 1980.

5. English ships driving on to a rocky shore in a gale. Canvas. 14½in. x 19½in. Signed C.V.V. At N.M.M.

Colour Plate 55. *Jan Griffier. A royal yacht and other shipping in a calm. This painting is beautifully done, with great attention to detail.* THE MUSEUM OF INNSBRUCK, AUSTRIA

Colour Plate 56.
Jan Griffier. A royal yacht saluting a large first-rate man-of-war. Fully signed. THE MUSEUM OF INNSBRUCK, AUSTRIA

Colour Plate 57. Peter Tillemans. The Prospect of the Thames at Twickenham with Pope's Villa.
BONHAMS

Chapter 9
Rare Painters

This chapter discusses six artists who occasionally painted marines but whose work is rare and seldom seen.

Jan Griffier
1651–1718

After being a pupil of such renowned masters as Rembrandt, van Ruysdael and Van de Velde, Jan Griffier made his way to England in the 1670s and stayed for forty years or so. He had a yacht, which (according to Grant[1]) he fitted up as an aquatic studio, and painted views from the river. He attempted a voyage to Rotterdam in his own yacht, but this ended in disaster as the boat was wrecked, carrying with her most of Griffier's savings. Nothing daunted, he built a new vessel and returned to England with her in 1687. Here, as well as being a painter, he became a map maker.

He is best remembered for his lively views of the Rhine Valley and he also did many copies of old masters. His English scenes are rarer, but one is in the Royal Collection, catalogued as 'A Prospect of Windsor Castle from the south, with horsemen and falconers in the foreground. Canvas. 21¼in. x 31½in. Signed and dated J. Griffier 1681'.

His marine pictures featuring ships are rarer still, but the National Maritime Museum has one of them and also two panorama pictures of Green Park and the river. The three paintings are:

1. Col. M.H. Grant. *The Old English Landscape Painters.*

1. View of the Queen's House, the Observatory and Greenwich on the river, with many ships. Canvas. 32in. x 52in. An early view, about 1675.

2. The same view, at approximately the same period. Canvas. 34in. x 51in.

3. A ketch-rigged royal yacht and the ship-rigged yacht *Peregrine* off Greenwich. Canvas. 45in. x 70in. A later view, probably about 1710. The ships are shown in great detail.

See Plate 40

The Museum of Innsbruck in Austria has two excellent ship portraits (Colour Plates 55 and 56). As might be expected from so good a painter, the quality of these two pictures is very good, the ships being shown very realistically and accurately.

Plate 40. Jan Griffier. Royal yachts off Greenwich. The 'ship-rigged' yacht in the middle is the Peregrine. *The yacht on the right is ketch rigged. In the background on the hill is the Royal Observatory with one of the towers of the Wren building in front.*

NATIONAL MARITIME MUSEUM

Plate 41. Peter Tillemans. *A view of Greenwich, about 1720.* OSCAR AND PETER JOHNSON

Peter Tillemans
1684–1734

This painter was born in Antwerp, a diamond cutter's son, and came to London, with his brother-in-law Peter Casteels, in 1708. He soon found employment in depicting the houses and estates of the nobility. Large canvases showing the horses, hounds and friends and relations in the country environs of a large rural estate became his speciality. But some of his most successful and attractive paintings were 'pure landscape', such as his 'View from Richmond Hill' and the equally famous 'View from Greenwich'.

Although Tillemans was not by any stretch of the imagination a marine painter, the rivers in his compositions often contain well drawn and pleasing little ship portraits. His views of Greenwich and Twickenham (Plate 41 and Colour Plate 57) are two good examples.

Colour Plate 58. *R. Woodcock. 'The Launch of a Fifty Gun Ship'. Canvas. 16½in. x 19¾in. Signed and dated R.W. Woodcock, 1727. This is an original composition, not a copy of a Van de Velde.*   SOTHEBY'S

Top right: **Colour Plate 59. Thomas Baston.** *This is one of the typical prints from the 'Bowles' album, from drawings by Thomas Baston.*   NATIONAL MARITIME MUSEUM

Bottom right: **Colour Plate 60. J. van Haeken.** *A pleasant coastal scene, with a large English man-of-war. This is one of the occasional seascapes done by Van Haeken.*   SOTHEBY'S

To His ROYAL HIGHNESS GEORGE PRINCE OF WALES.

Baston F. *J. Harris S.*

Plate 42. R. Woodcock. *The* Royal William *becalmed. Signed and dated 1720. This is an almost exact copy of Van de Velde the Younger's picture of the* Royal Sovereign *of 1704, with minor alterations to the flags and the stern!*   NATIONAL MARITIME MUSEUM

Plate 43. R. Woodcock. A battle between the English and the Dutch. It is based entirely on Van de Velde's great painting of the Gouden Leeuw *going into action at the Battle of the Texel, in 1673. The central ship has been made into an English flagship, mainly by altering the flags. (See Archibald,* Dictionary of Sea Painters.) NATIONAL MARITIME MUSEUM

Robert Woodcock
1692-1728

Robert Woodcock was an Admiralty clerk who developed a keen interest in drawing ships. At the age of thirty he took up oil painting and, as he was a great admirer of the Van de Veldes, he made copies of their works. He had only six years between taking up oil painting and his early death in 1728, aged thirty-six, but the few of his more mature paintings we have are very good and, like Brooking, his premature death robbed us of a great marine artist.

There are three of his paintings in the National Maritime Museum at Greenwich, and there was one in the Mellon Collection at Yale. The latter was a remarkably good one entitled 'The Launch of a Fifty Gun Ship' and it was signed and dated 1727. It was later sold at Sotheby's as Lot 85 in the Mellon Sale on 18 November 1981 (see Colour Plate 58). His copies of Van de Velde works are so direct and exact and 'in period' that it is difficult to be sure who did them, unless they are signed. Fortunately he did sign some of his later works, either in full – R. Woodcock – or in monogram R.V. (according to Archibald[2]). As he was painting well after 1707, most of the ships in his pictures wear the post 1707 red ensign (i.e. with the St. George's cross and St. Andrew's cross superimposed on a blue ground in the 'fly' of the ensign).

2. E.H.H. Archibald. *Dictionary of Sea Painters*. Antique Collectors' Club, 2nd 1989.

To his *ROYAL HIGHNESS* GEORGE *PRINCE* of *WALES*,
This PLATE of his MAI^{TIES} SHIP the ROYAL GEORGE
is most humbly *Inscribed*.

T. Baston delin: *S. Cole Sculp.*

Plate 44. Thomas Baston. *Another typical Baston print.* NATIONAL MARITIME MUSEUM

Thomas Baston
First quarter of the eighteenth century

In 1723, Thomas Bowles published an album of 'Twenty-two prints of several of the capital ships of His Majesty's Royal Navy with a variety of other sea pieces after the drawings of T. Baston'. Two of the drawings are in the National Maritime Museum at Greenwich, and the author saw another many years ago at auction at Sotheby's. Apart from these, no other drawings or oil paintings by him are known.

Jean Baptist Bouttats
Fl. prior to 1700 and died after 1738

This Flemish artist, born in Antwerp, is known mainly from his landscapes, views of houses, game and bird pictures. He also did copies of earlier pictures, and painted coats of arms. He was a Master in the Antwerp Guild in 1706. Examples of his work are in Leipzig and Dresden. His pictures also turn up in England, mostly dated in the 1720s and 1730s, from which it might be presumed that he also visited England rather late in life. In England his work seems to have taken on a marine flavour.

The National Maritime Museum, Greenwich, has two pictures by him. The first is entitled 'The Arrival of Charles II at the Hague, 15th May, 1660, on his way to England'. It is signed and dated 1738, and is thought to be a copy of an earlier picture or engraving. The second is a straight-forward little seascape showing a sixth-rate saluting a state barge. It also is

Plate 45. J.B. Bouttats. *A calm coastal scene showing a Dutch smalschip and a States yacht. Signed and dated 1735.*   BRIAN KOETSER

Plate 46. J.B. Bouttats. A calm coastal scene with a States yacht and other small boats. Signed and dated 172?
PHILLIPS

signed. The whole is painted rather heavily, and the figures are rather wooden and too big for the ships they occupy.

There is also a signed and dated (1730) work by him at Shipley Art Gallery, Gateshead.

During the last twenty years or so two marine scenes have turned up on the English art market. The first one (Plate 45) was in the possession of the dealer Brian Koetser in 1967, was signed and dated (1735) and, as is evident from the photograph, was a quite attractive little picture. The second one (Plate 46) was a very similar little scene which appeared at Phillips in the late 1970s. It also is signed and dated (172?). Both pictures are of an estuary scene, probably in Holland.

The author has been unable to trace any further marine pictures by him.

Joseph van Haeken
1699-1749

There is a sprinkling of quite decorative but otherwise rather indifferent paintings of calm seascapes from the early years of the eighteenth century which are signed J. v. Haeken. It seems most likely that these were one-off efforts by Joseph van Haeken who was a Flemish painter born in Antwerp in 1699. He came to England in 1719 and was employed mainly as a 'drapery' painter by some of the eminent portrait painters of the period, such as Thomas Hudson and Alan Ramsey. However, it is recorded that he started his career in England as a young man by painting 'History and Genre pieces' which probably included an occasional seascape. He also painted a series of 'fish portraits' for the Fishmongers Hall in London where they are still hanging. He died in England in 1749.

The painting illustrated in Colour Plate 60 is a coastal scene with an English man-of-war. It is on canvas, 24in. x 33in. and is signed lower centre 'J.V.Haek…'. It was sold at Sotheby's on 7 December 1994, Lot 113. Another example is recorded in Archibald's book, but his paintings of seascapes and ships are very rare.

Epilogue

The Embarkation of Henry VIII and his retinue at Dover for the 'Field of the Cloth of Gold' in 1520

It is perhaps appropriate to close this book about early marine artists working in England with a brief consideration of this picture (Plate 47), in the Royal Collection at Hampton Court, which is certainly the earliest marine picture in England depicting an entirely English occasion.

A very good and full description and history of this picture is given in Sir Oliver Millar's catalogue of *The Tudor, Stuart and early Georgian Pictures in the Collection of Her Majesty the Queen*, 1963, No. 24, page 54. The origin of the picture is shrouded in mystery, as it is not really certain exactly when or where it was painted. Millar's opinion is that it was probably done some considerable time after 1520, probably as late as 1540, by an unknown Flemish artist (or several artists, as the figures and the ships were probably done by different hands).

The view of Dover is from the south-west point of the harbour, so the two forts in the foreground would be the 'Archcliff' and the 'Black Bulwarks'. On the left in the background is Dover Castle. The five principal vessels shown all fly streamers with the St. George's cross and are decorated by shields bearing the St. George's cross and Tudor emblems. The King is seen standing on the deck of the fourth ship, slightly further away from the foreground of the picture, and this is presumed to be the *Great Harry.* The ships have in fact not been positively identified, but they do give a very true picture of the great galleons of the early sixteenth century, with their towering stern castles and fore castles, and often with four masts. They look rather unstable, judging by this picture, and it is perhaps not surprising that the *Mary Rose,* when overloaded with extra guns and crew, heeled over and sank in the Solent in 1545.

It is interesting to compare these early pictures with those of about one hundred to one hundred and fifty years later which are described in this book. The early ones are basically commemorative and put together without much regard for a true record of the appearance of the event. One hundred and fifty years later the artists are striving after realism aided by more understanding of perspective and immensely better painting technique. They also understood more about seamanship and the actual construction and rigging of the great ships they were illustrating. This trend culminated in the great realist school of the seventeenth century Dutch painters such as Simon de Vlieger and the Van de Veldes who could put any ship in any sort of weather on to canvas and it would look right.

Plate 47. *The embarkation of Henry VIII and his retinue at Dover for the 'Field of the Cloth of Gold' in 1520, by an unknown artist.*

THE ROYAL COLLECTION – HER MAJESTY THE QUEEN

INDEX

Names in italics are names of ships
Page numbers in bold type refer to illustrations and captions